Inky Expressions

Coloring Book For Everyone

DRAWINGS BY KIMBERLY GARVEY

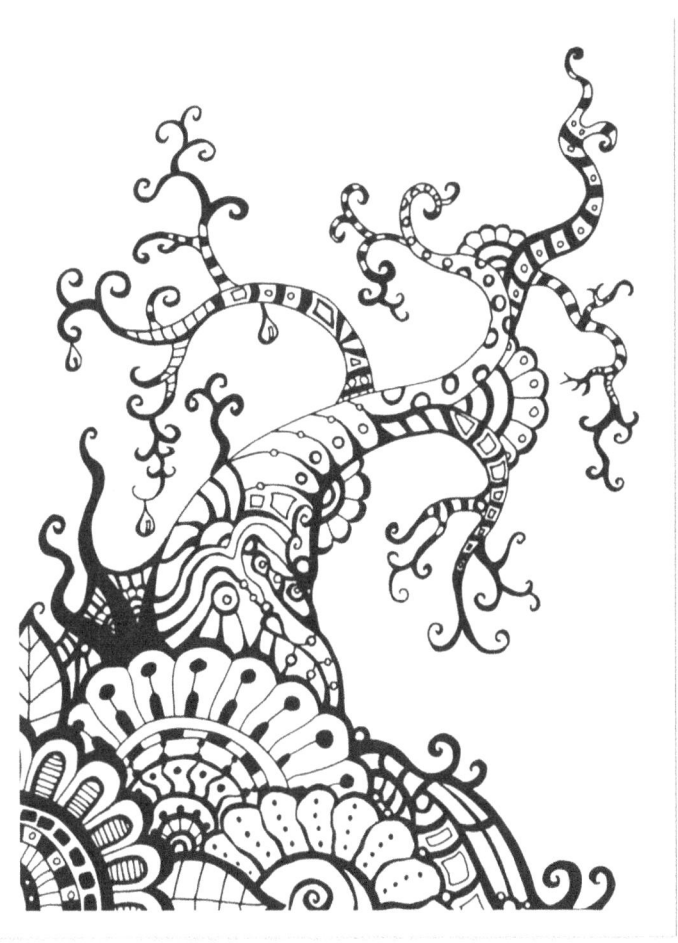

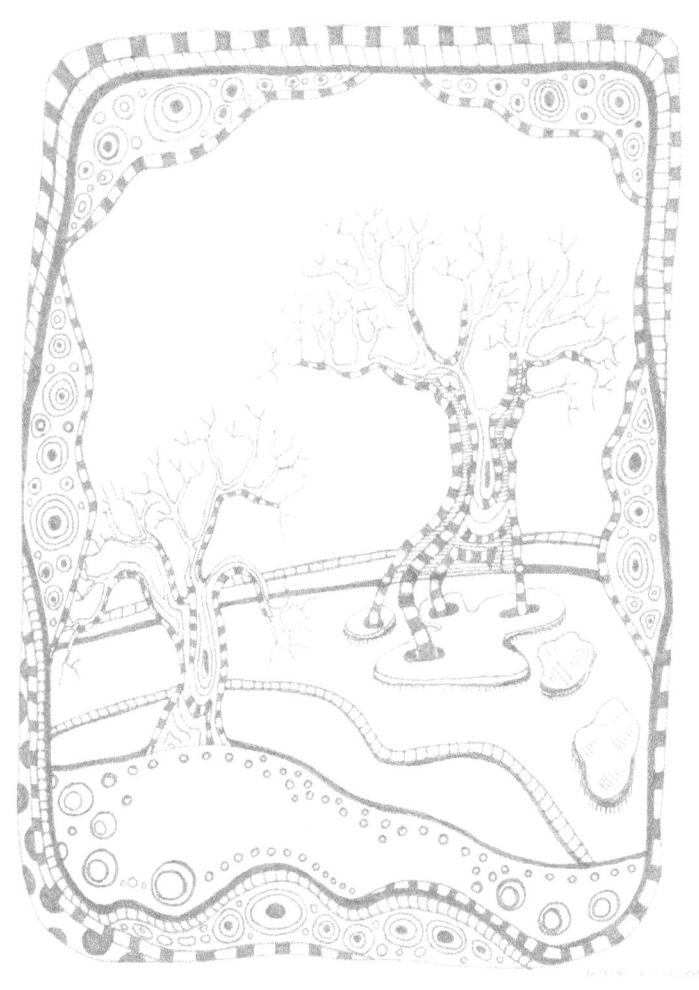

WARNING!!!!

Please put a protection sheet of paper between the pages when using markers to prevent bleed-through.

A protection sheet is included at the back of this book.

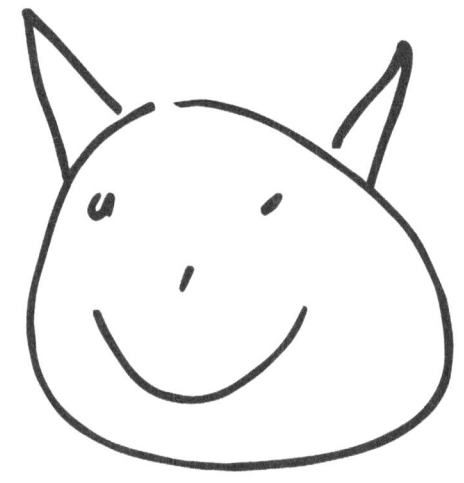

KIMBERLYGARVEY.COM

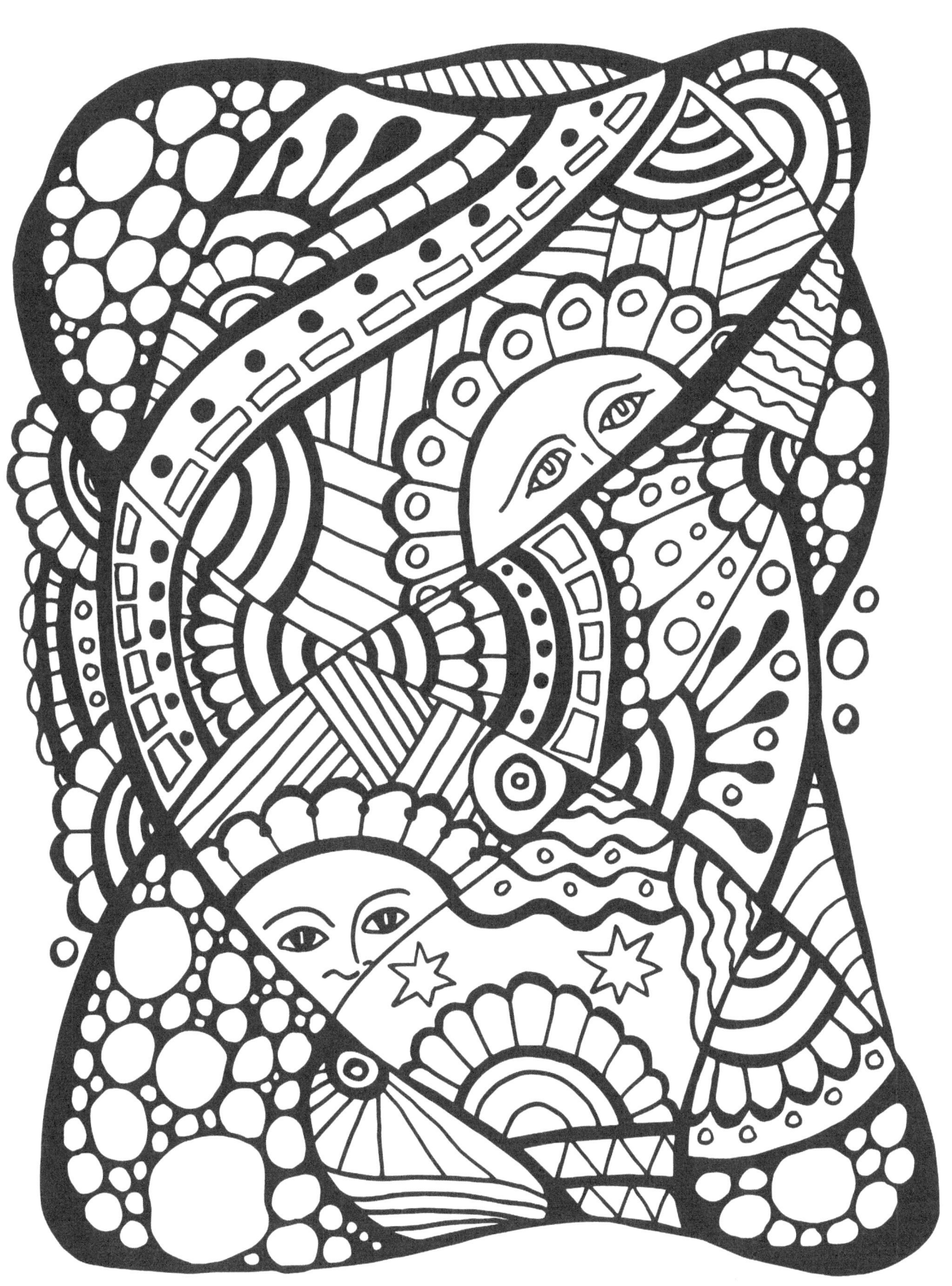

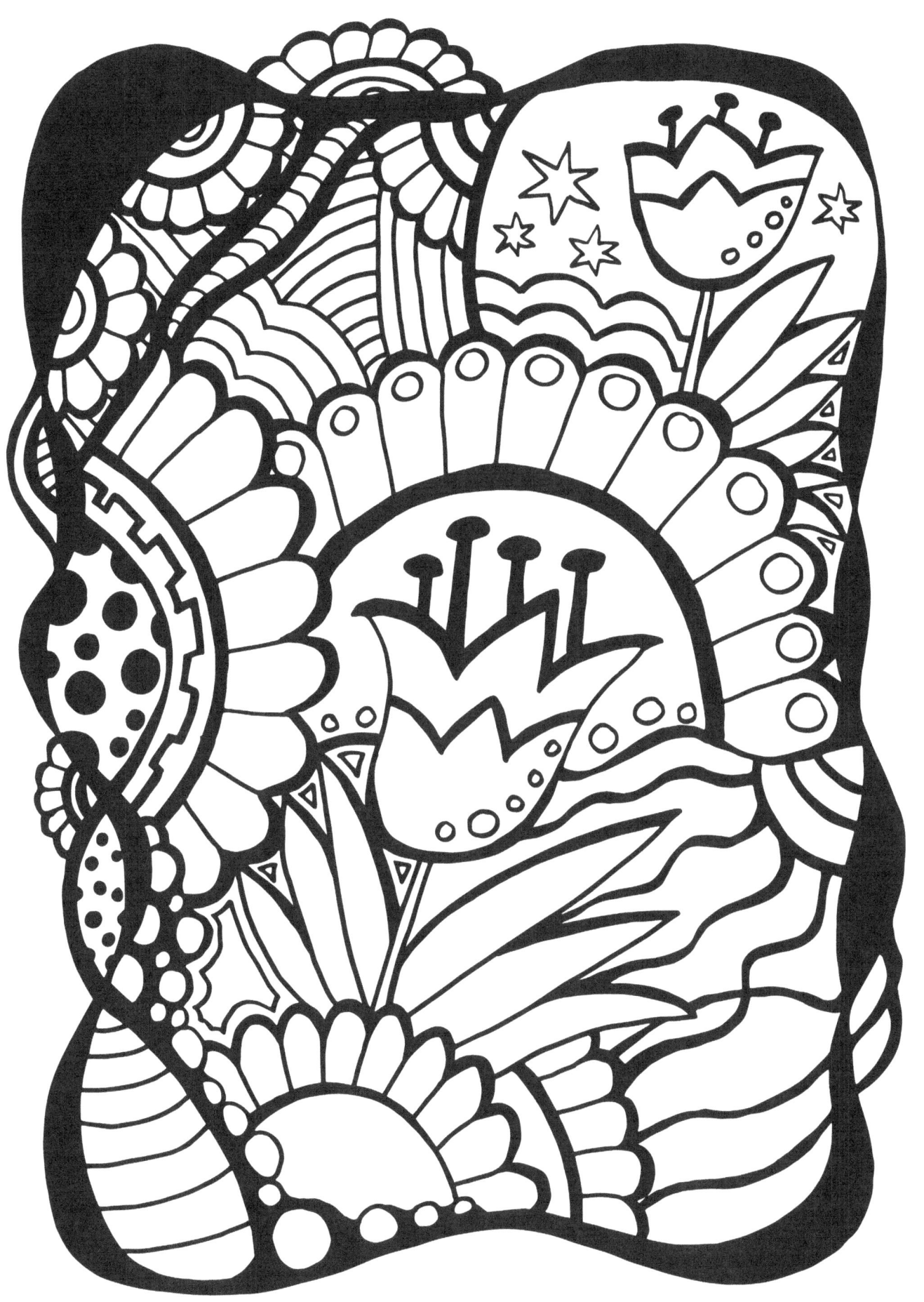

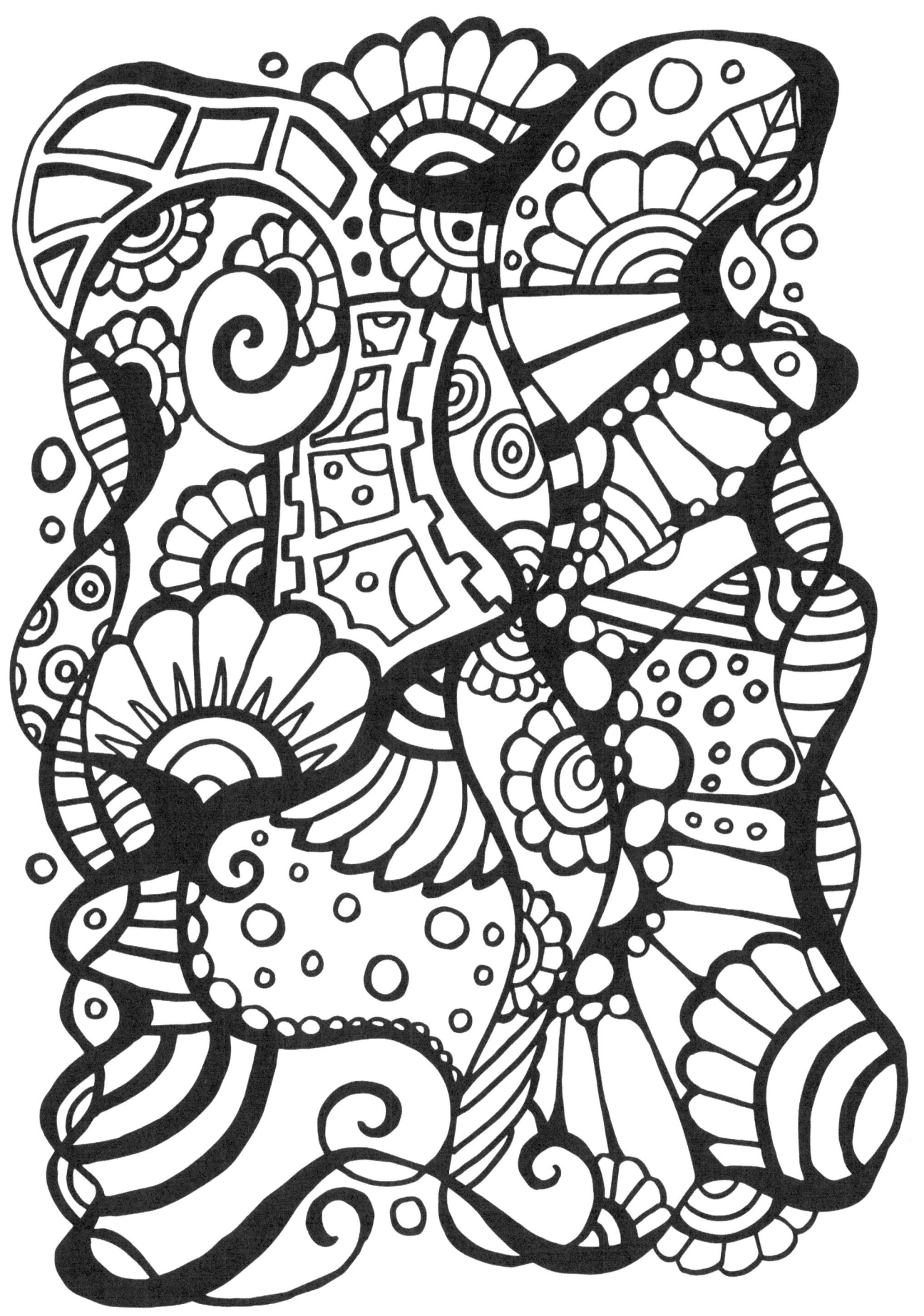

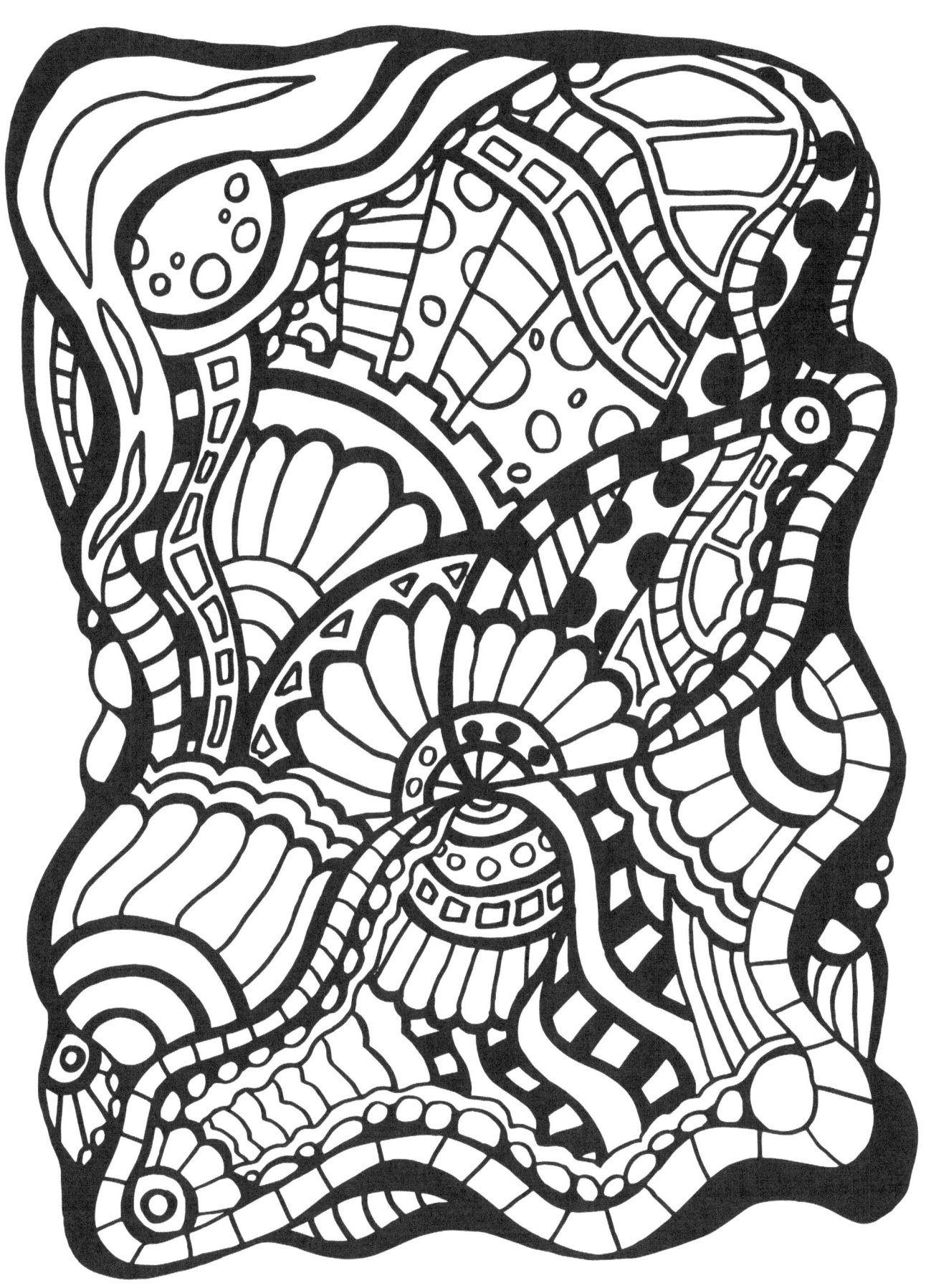

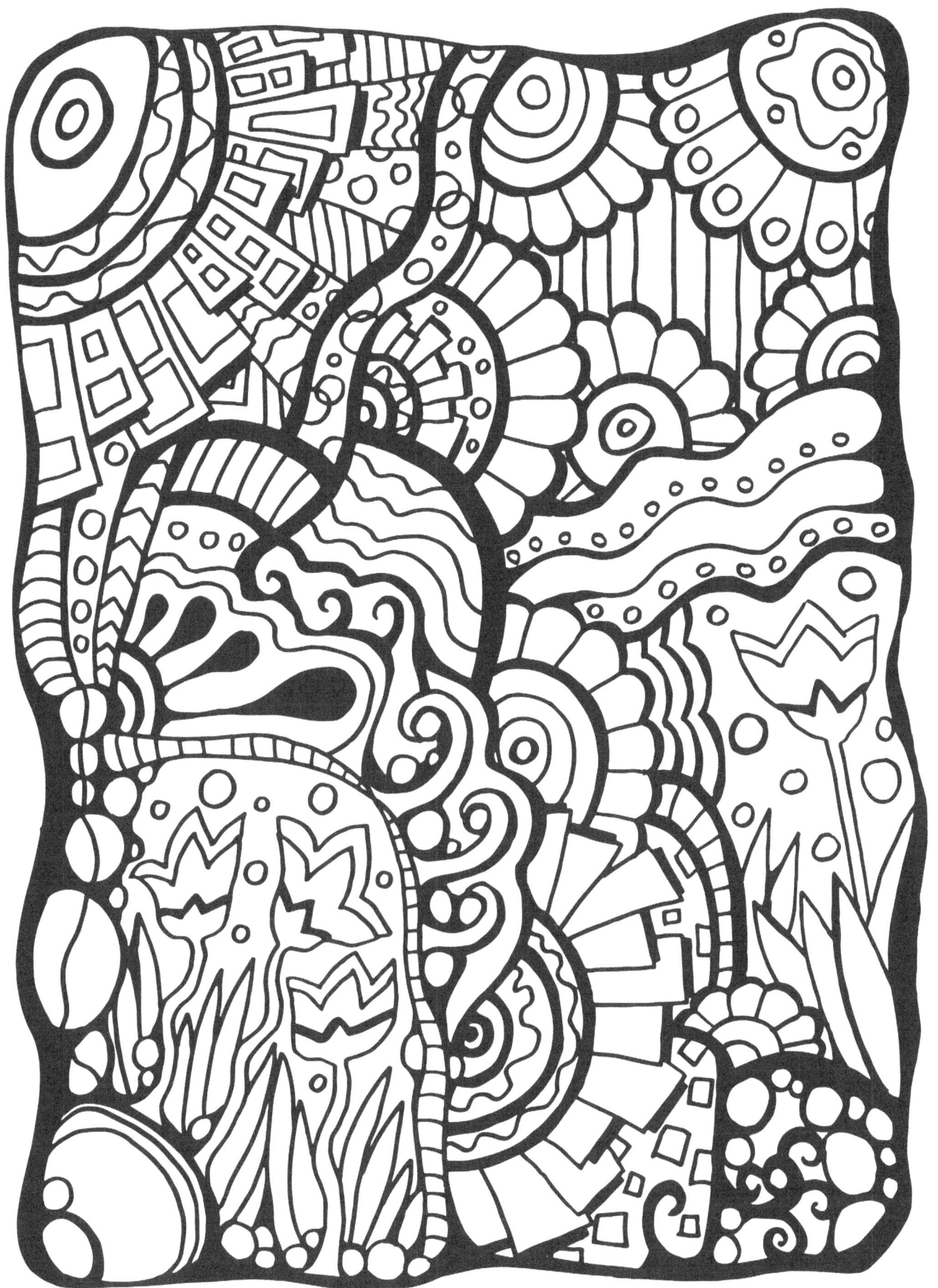

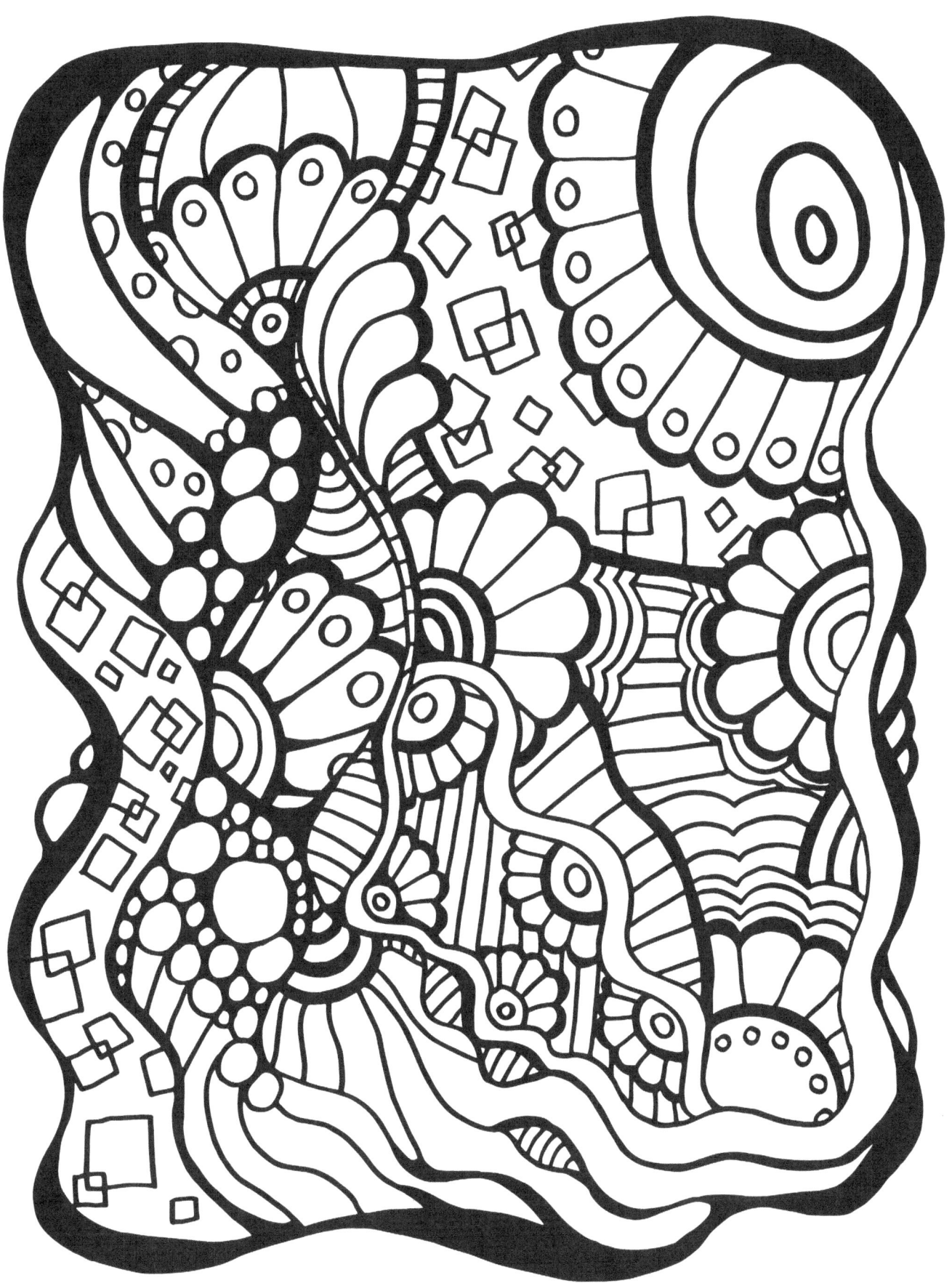

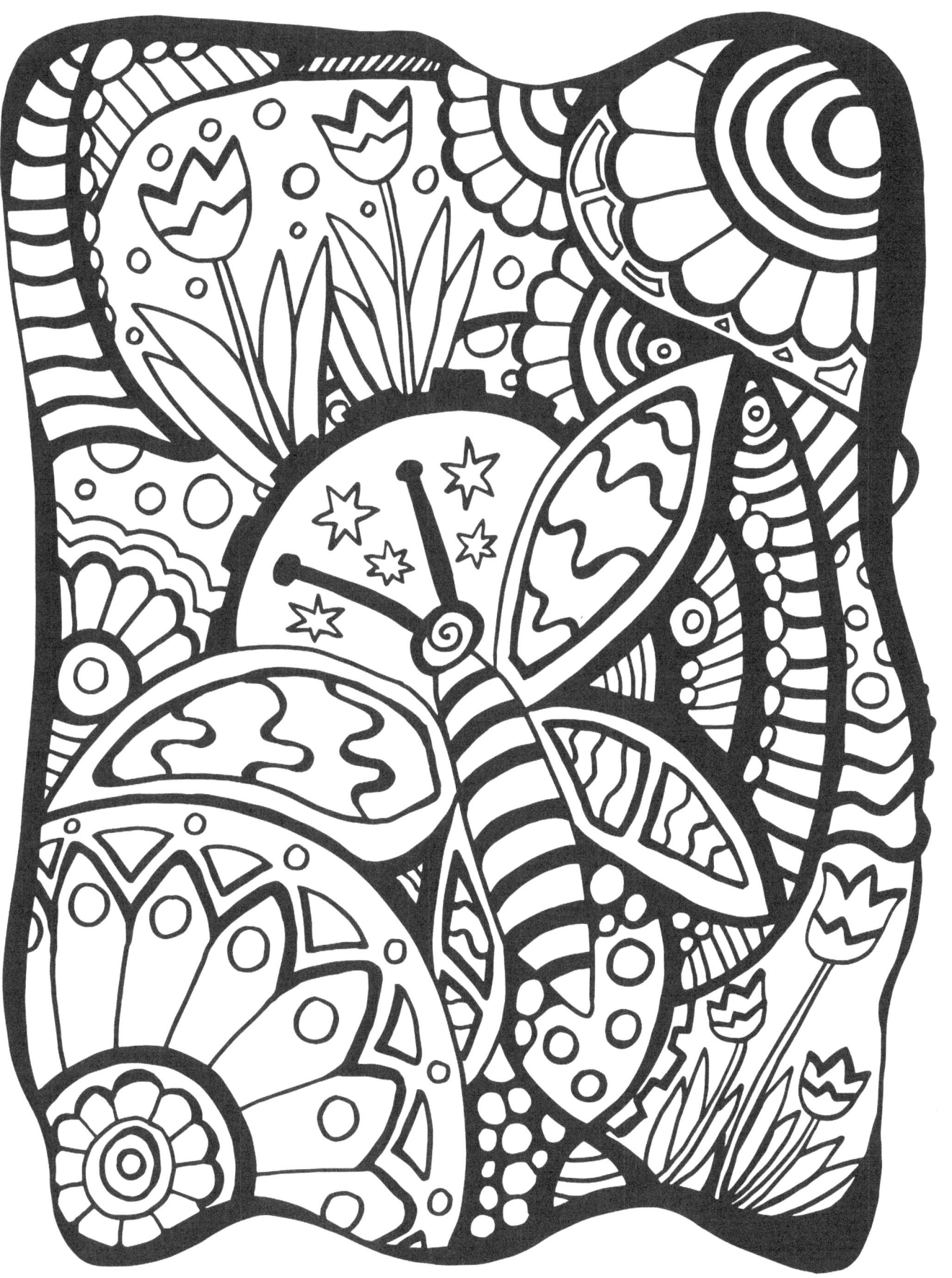

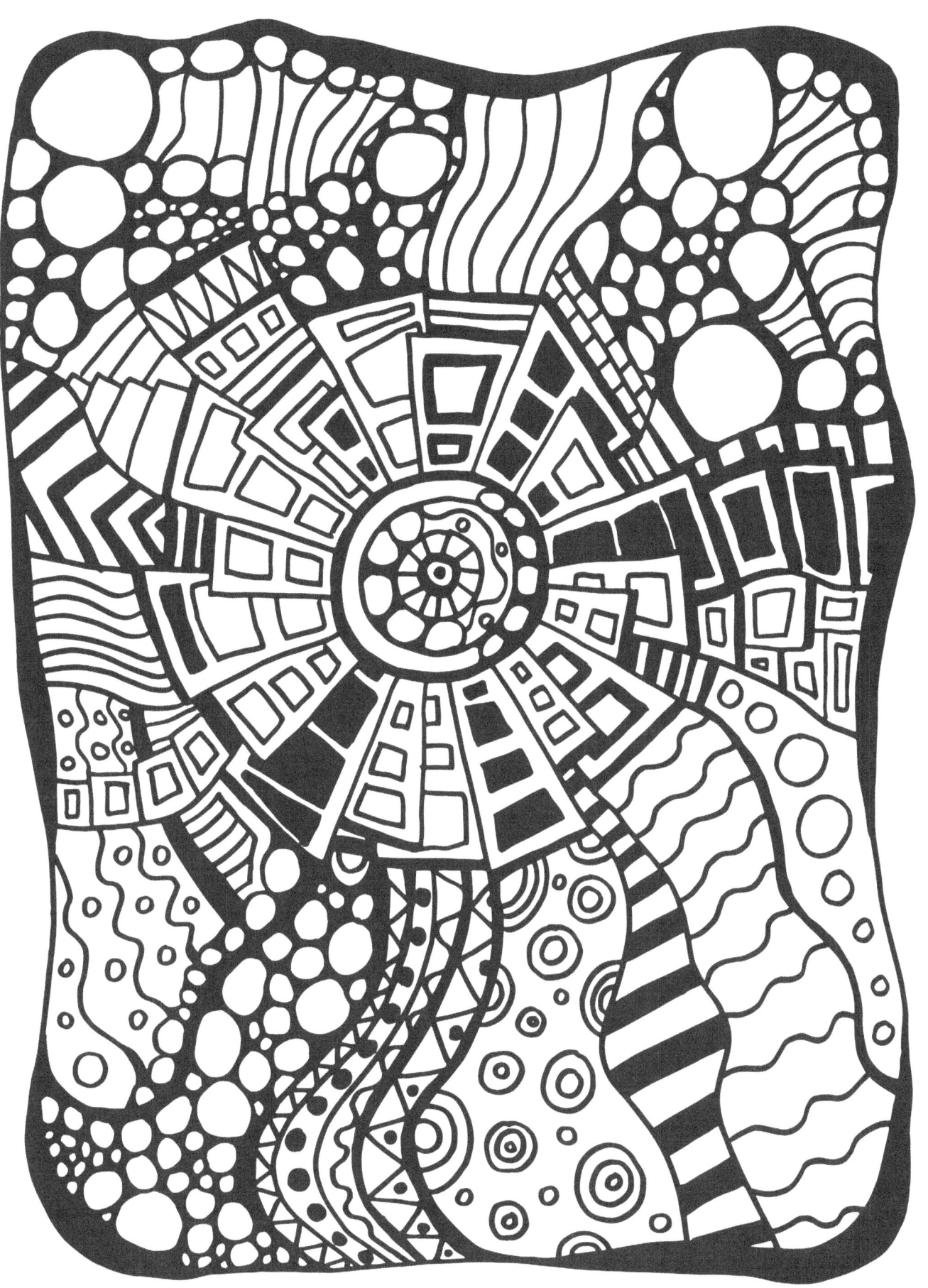

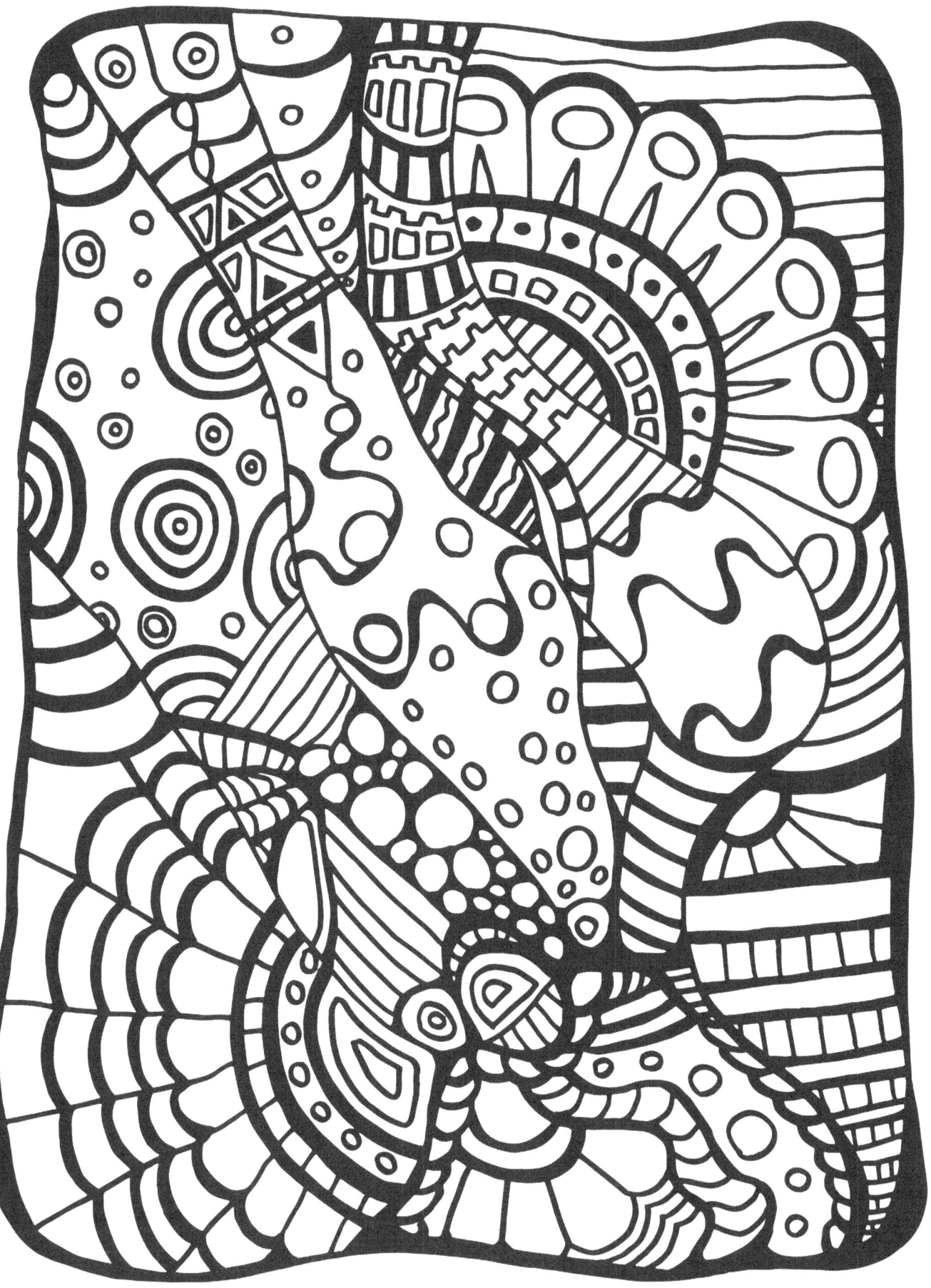

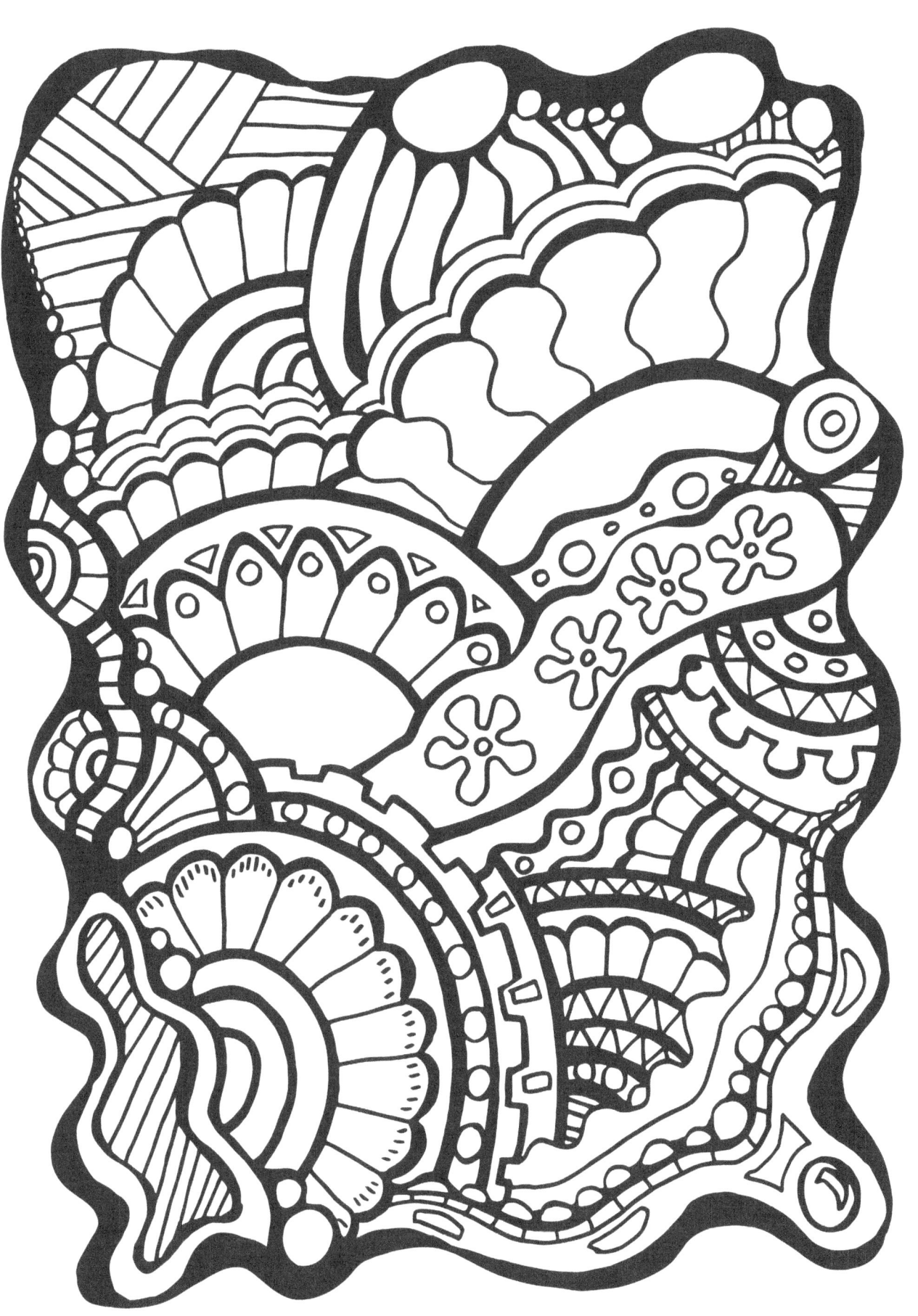

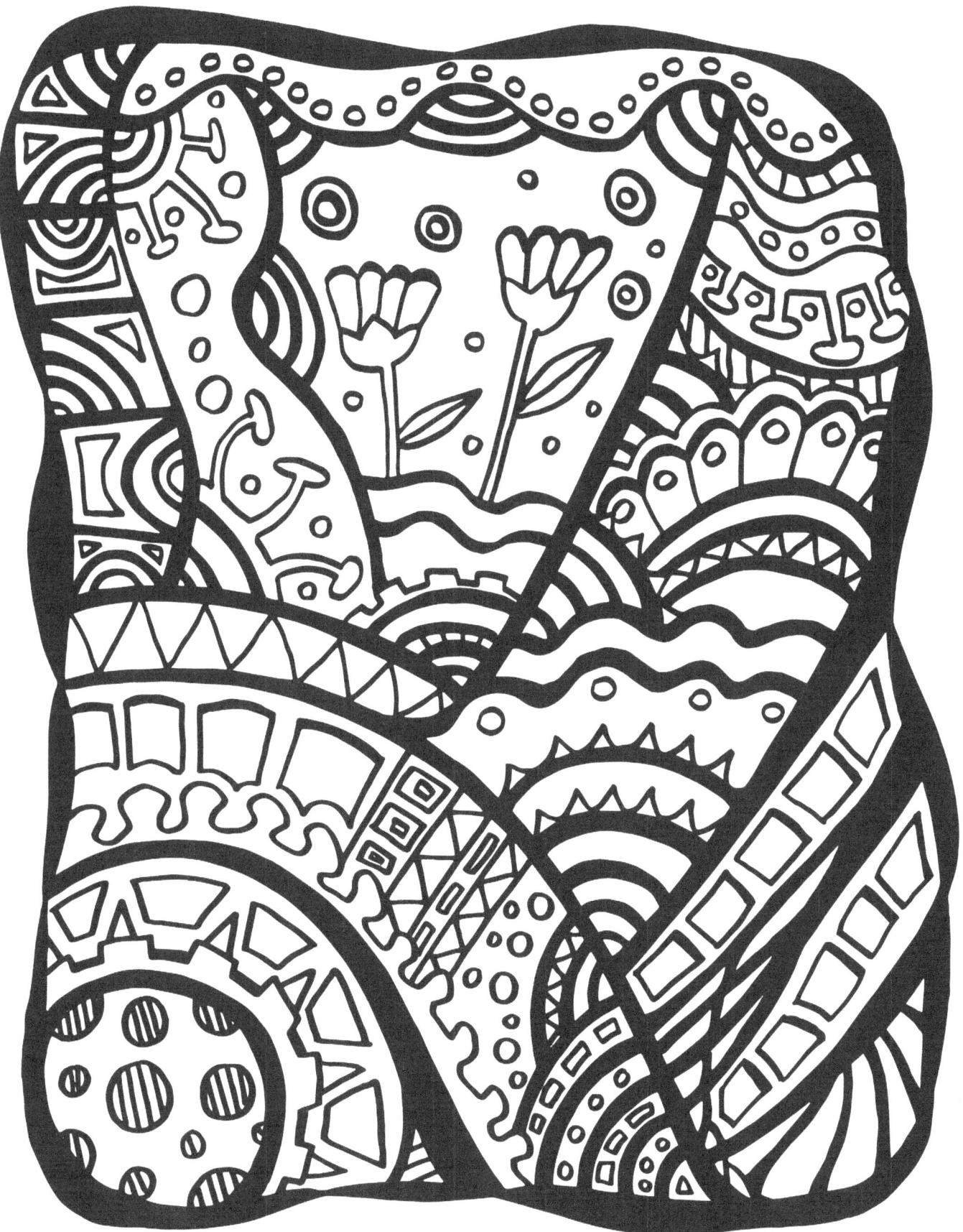

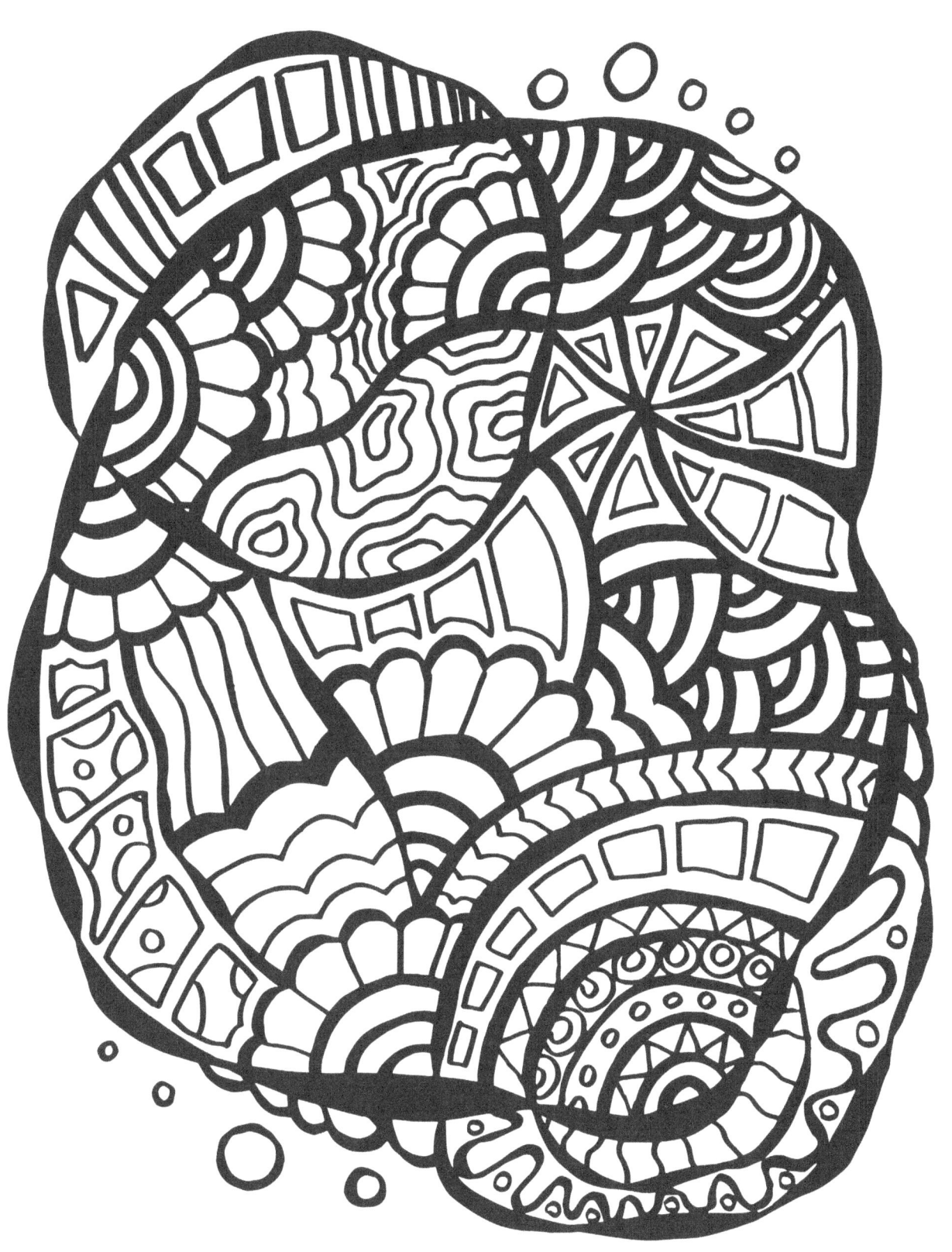

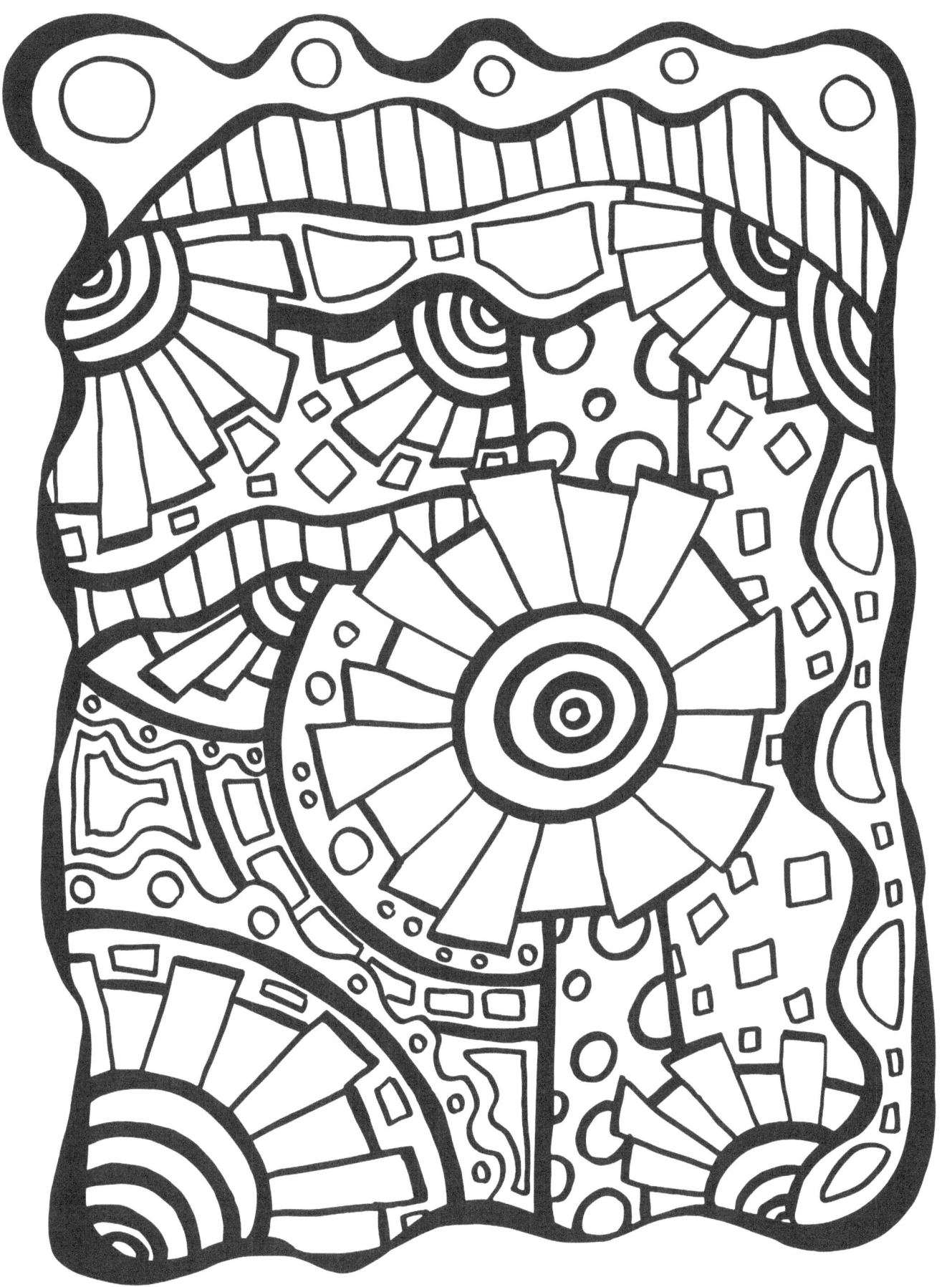

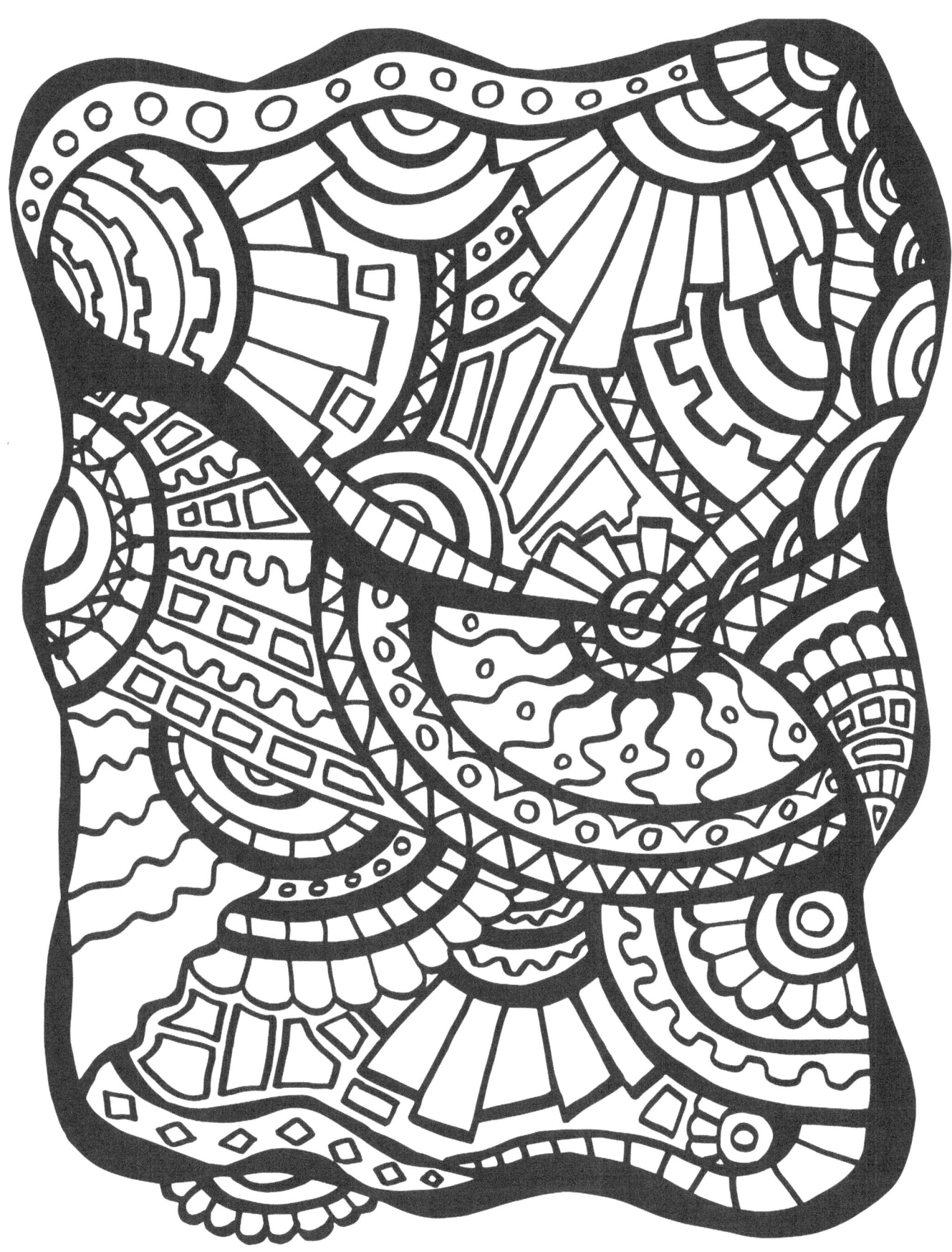

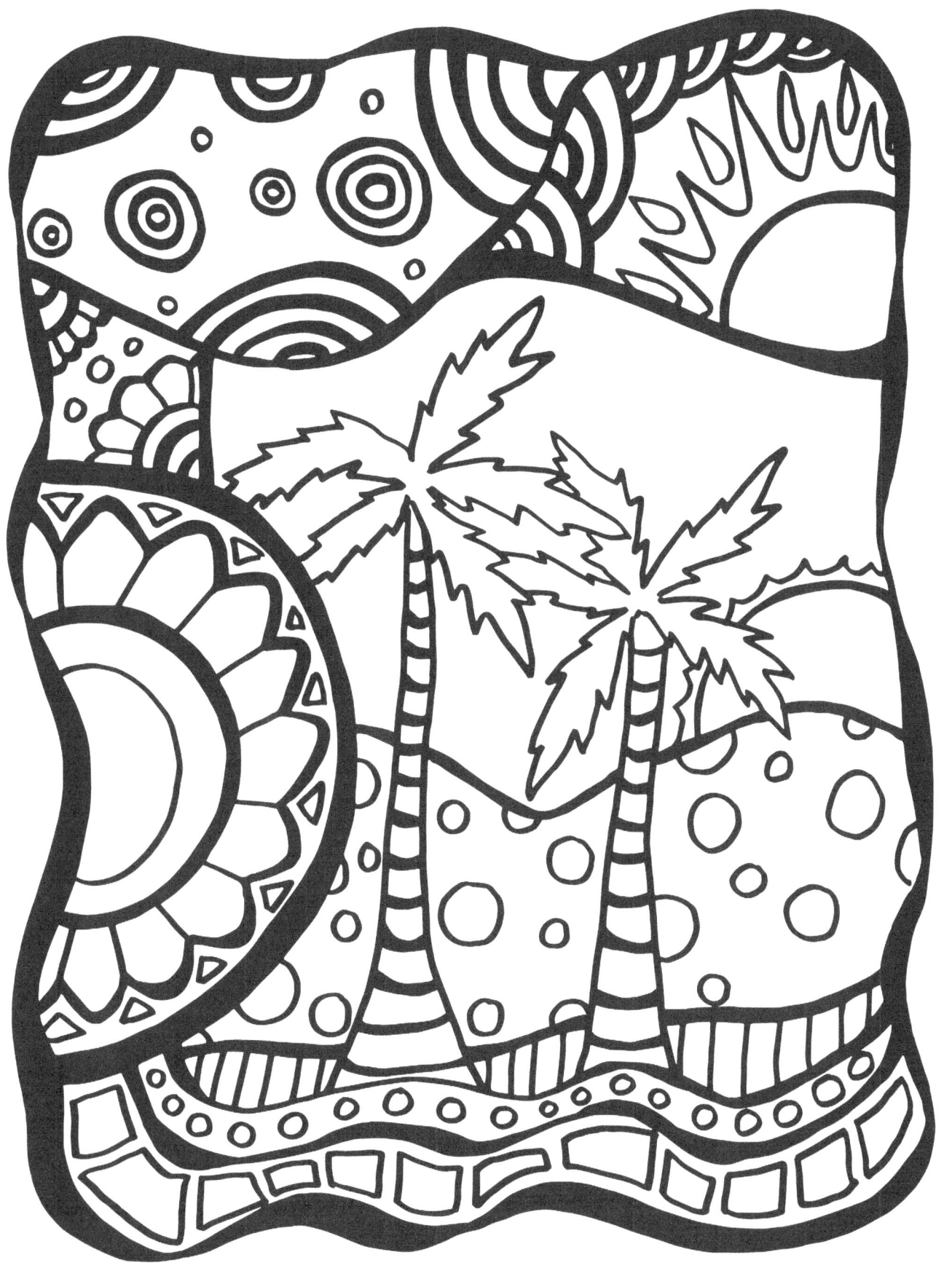

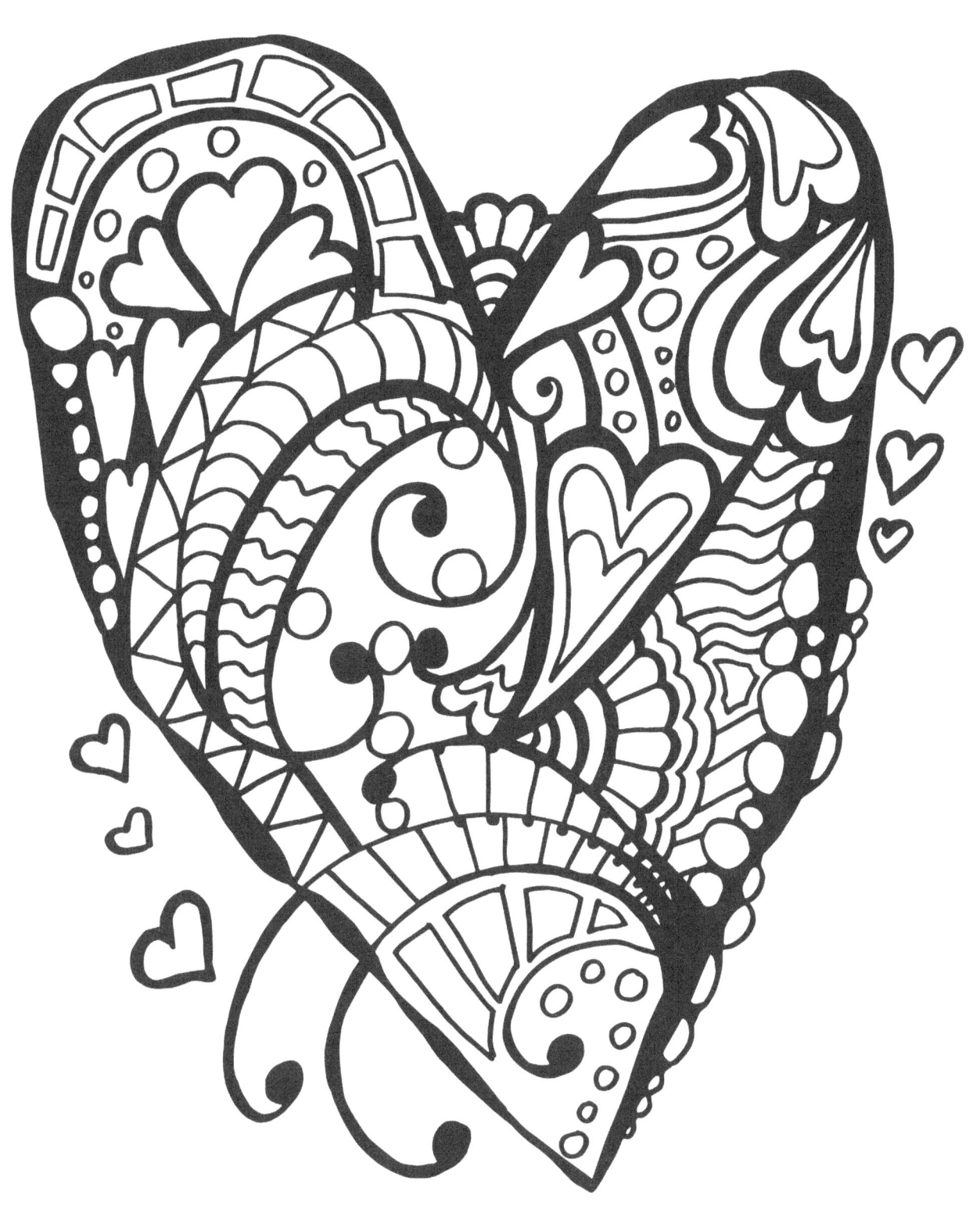

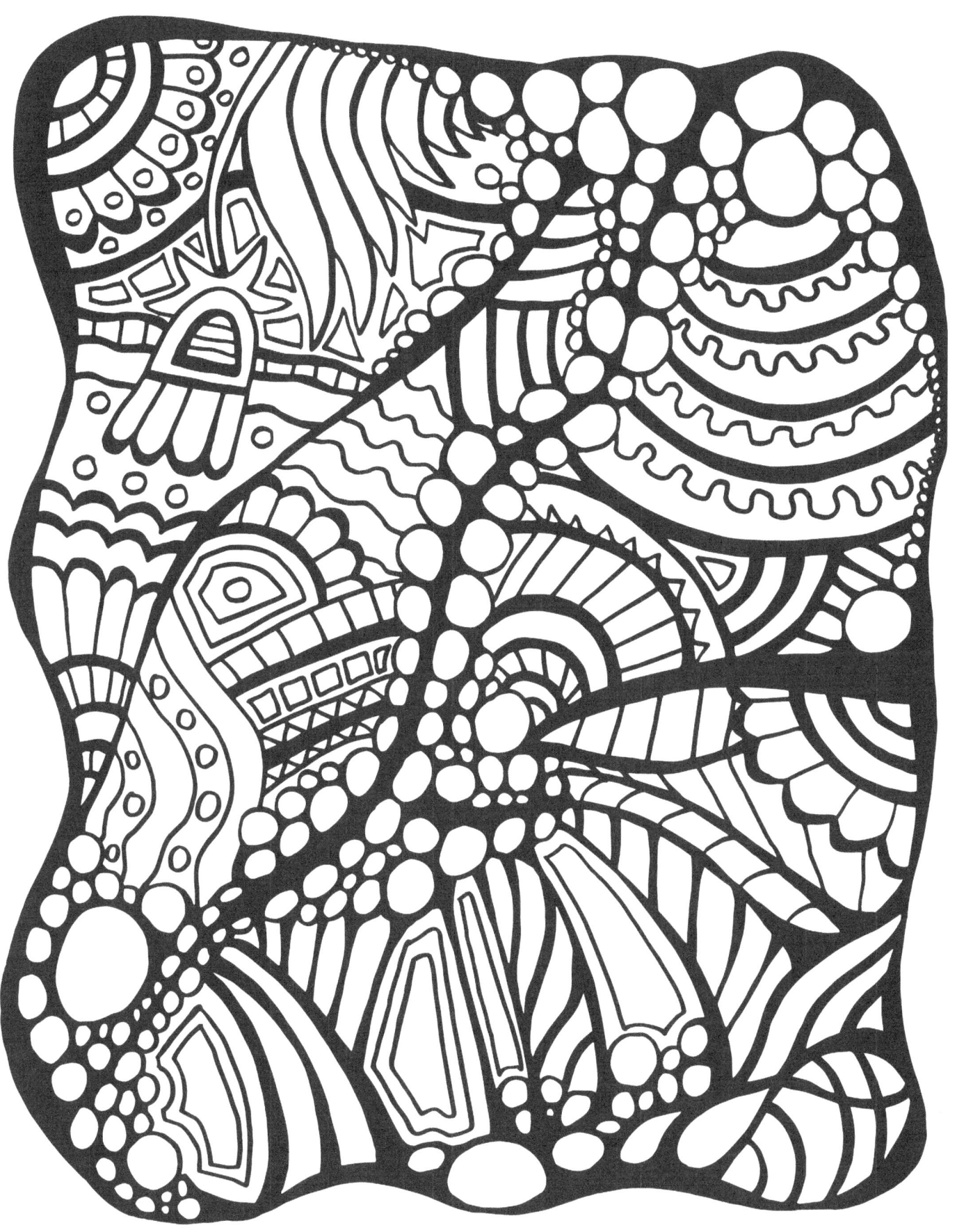

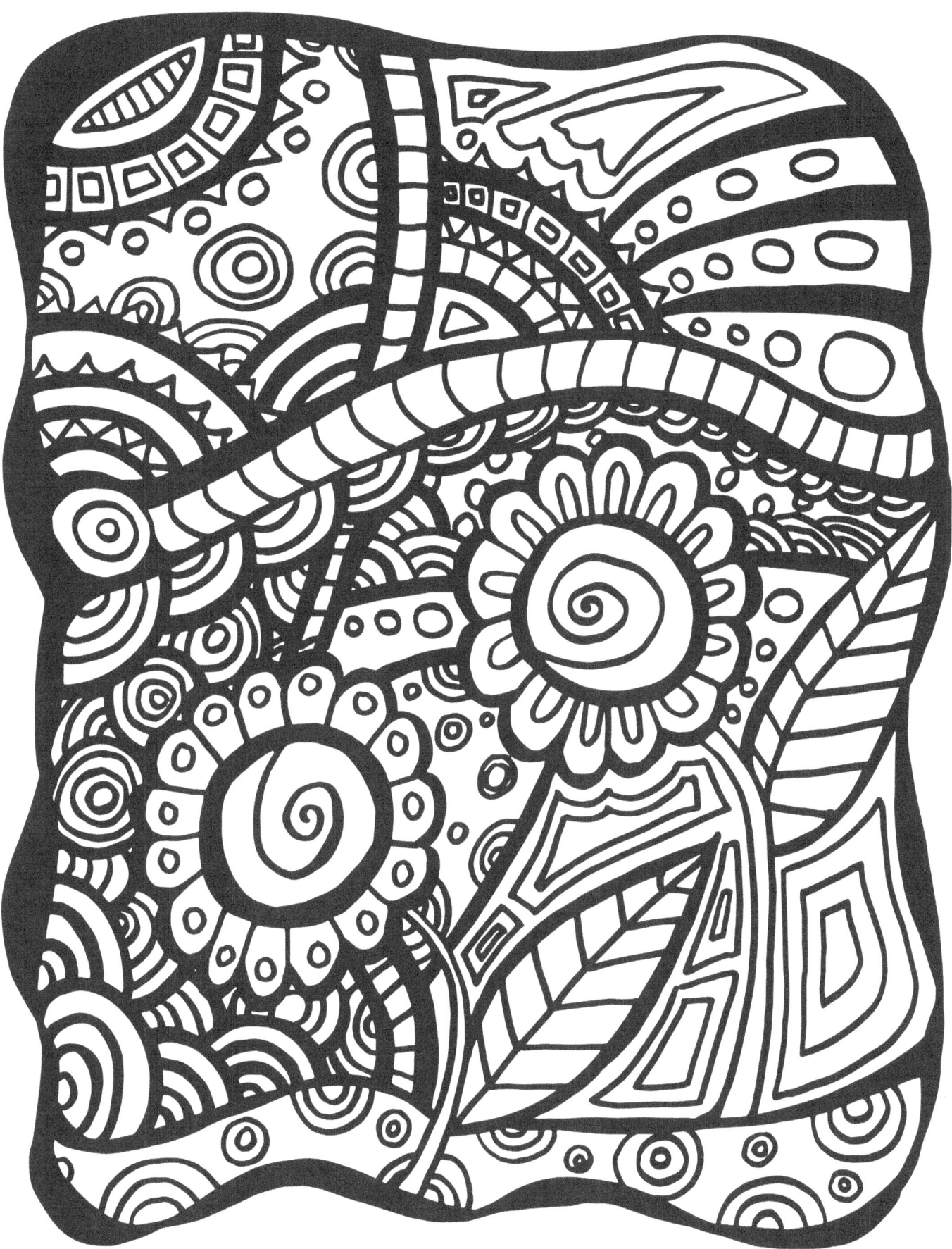

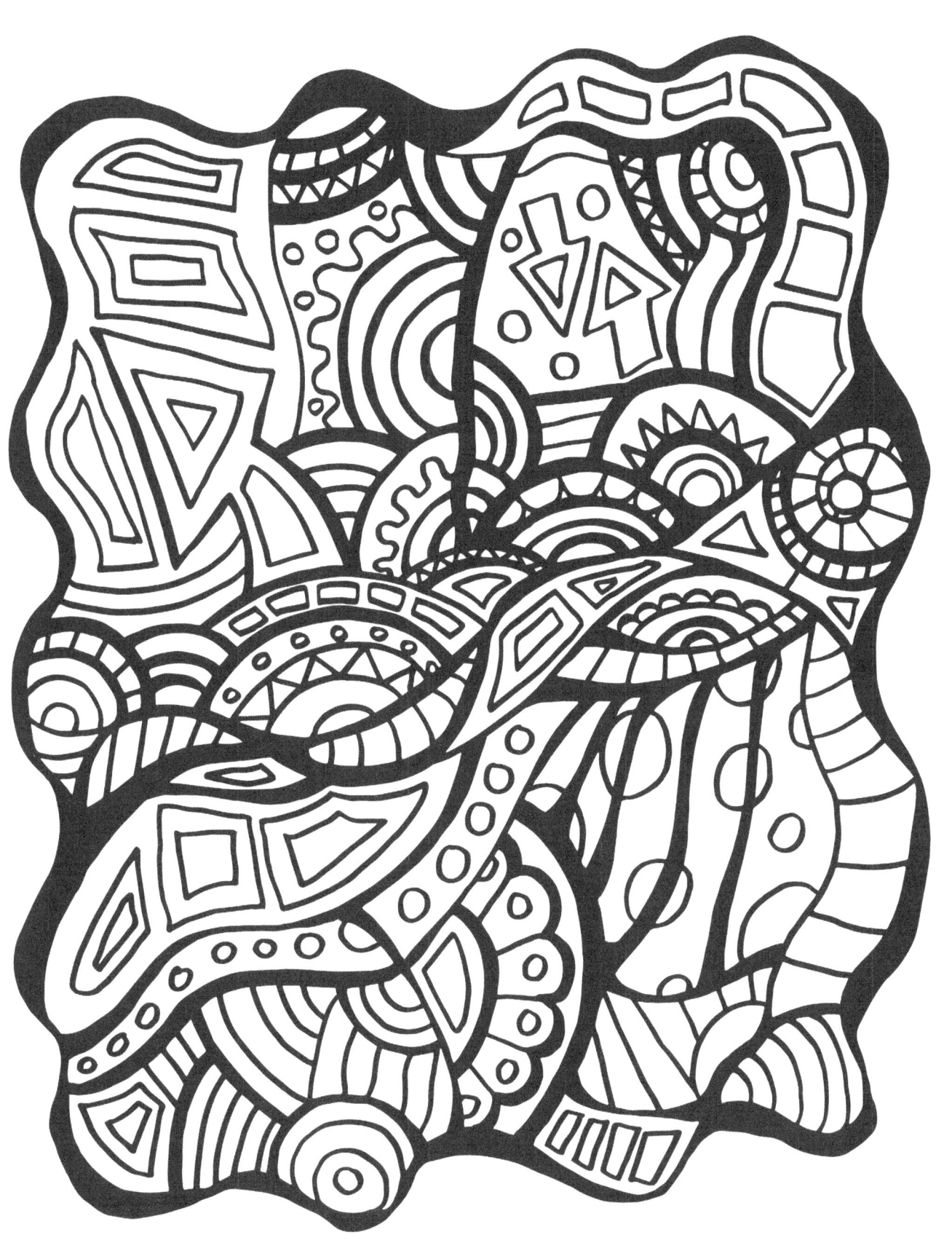

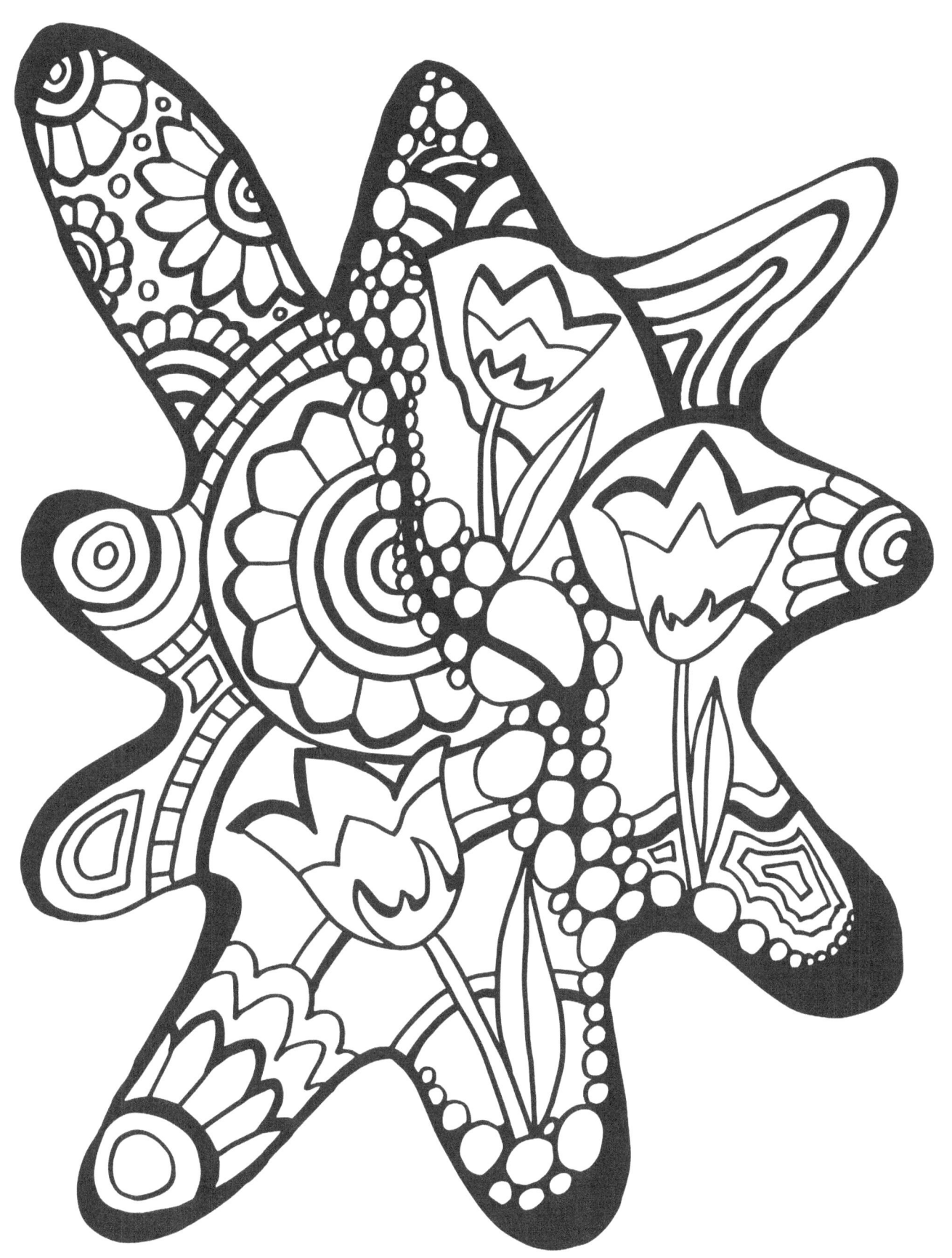

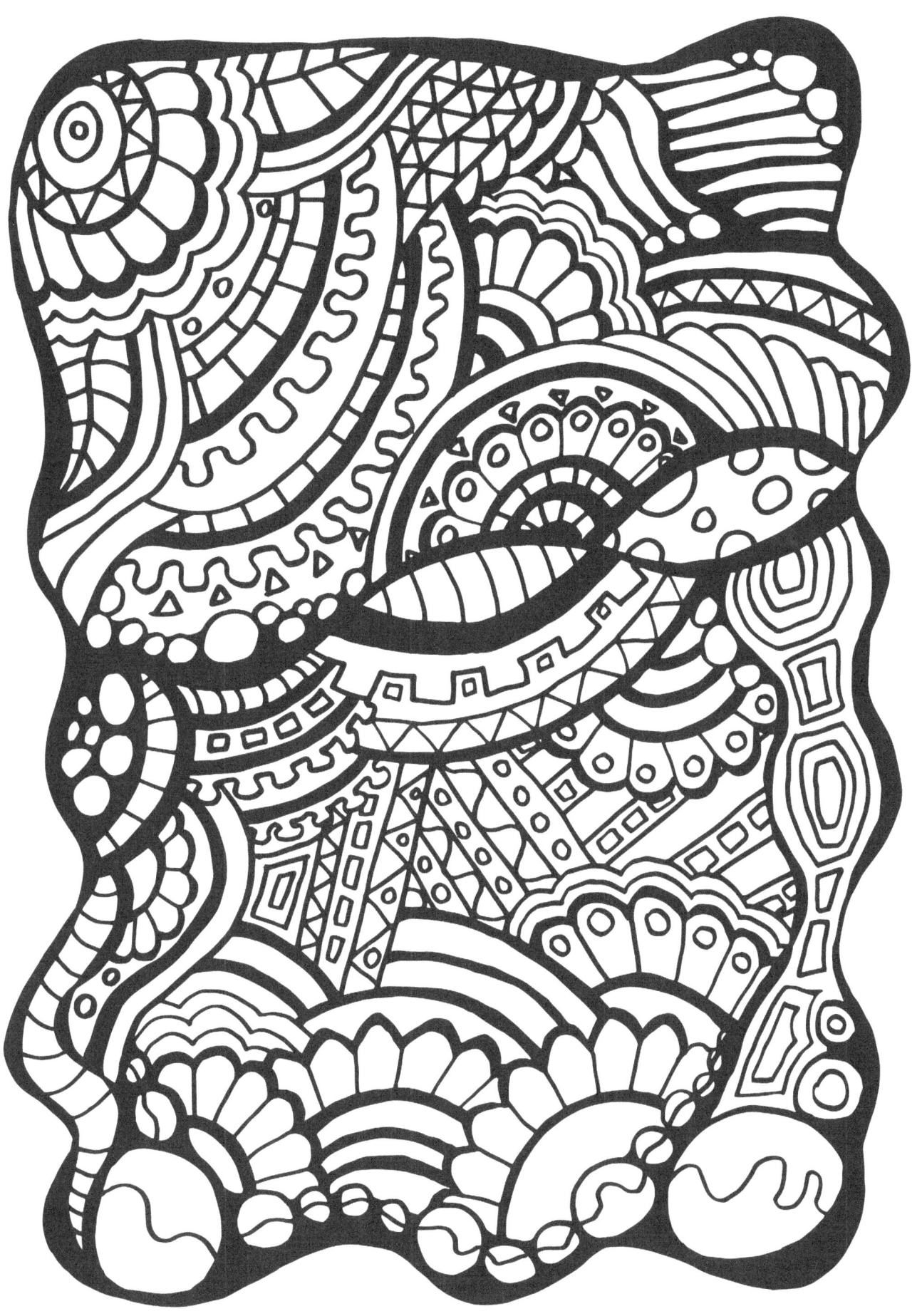

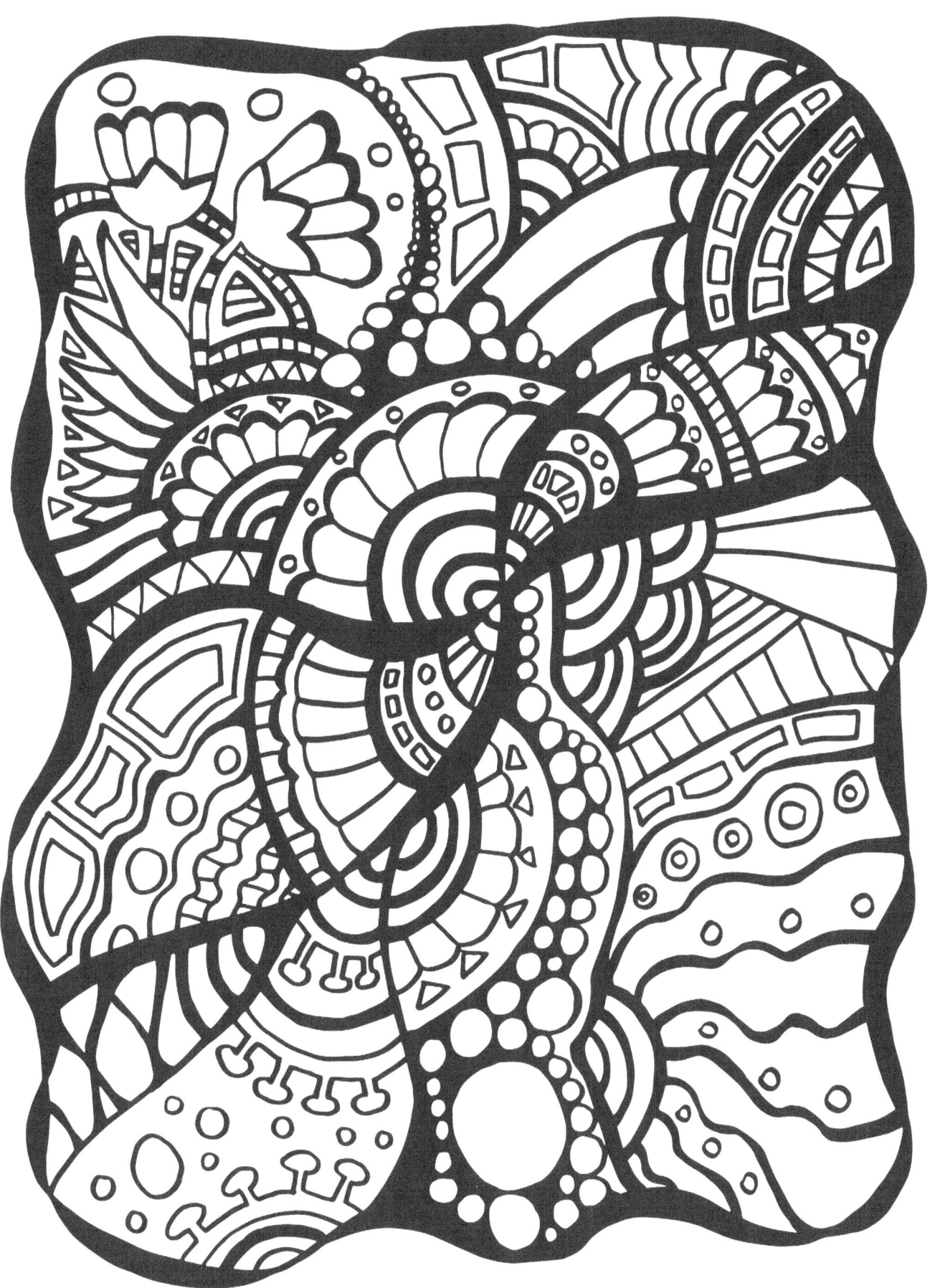

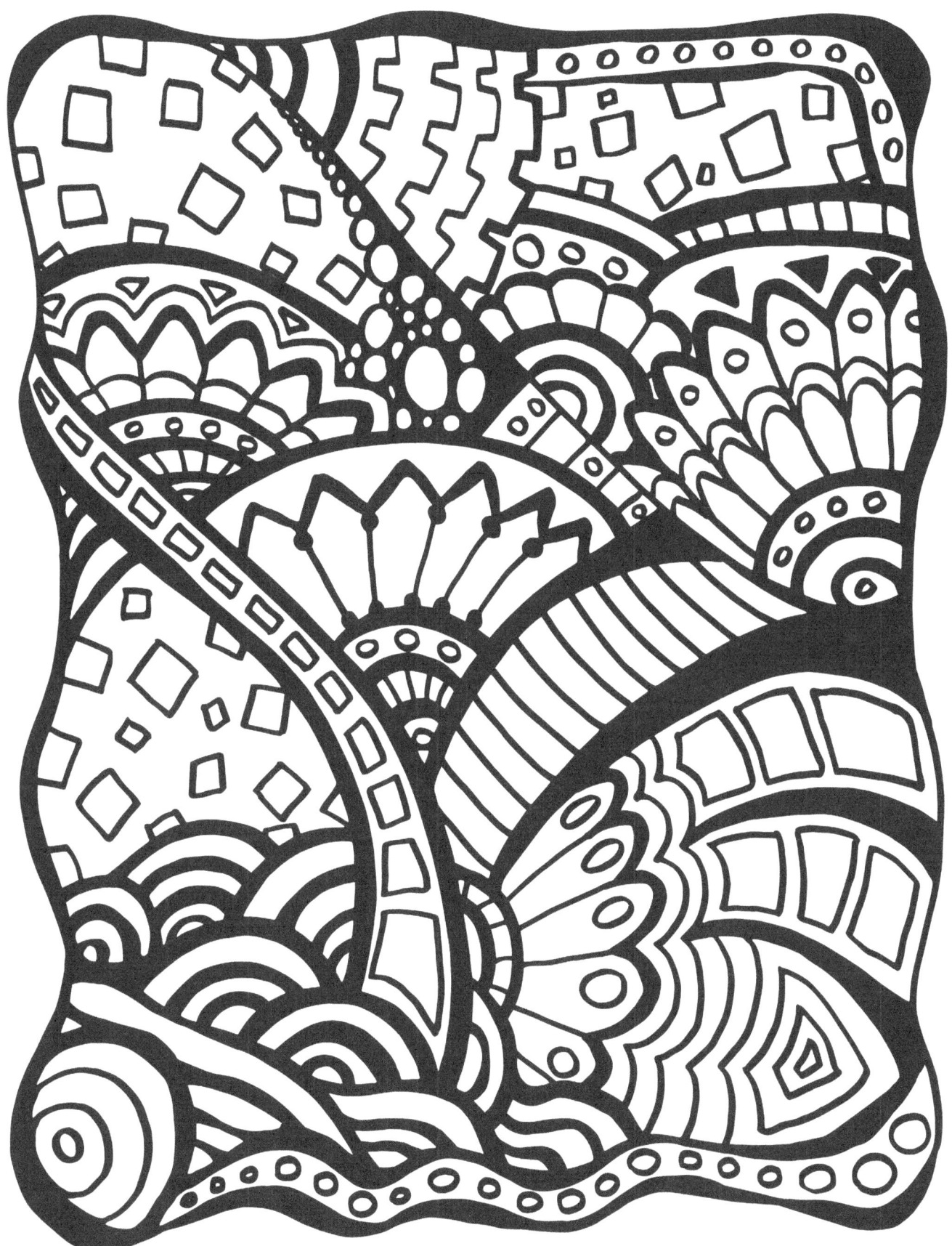

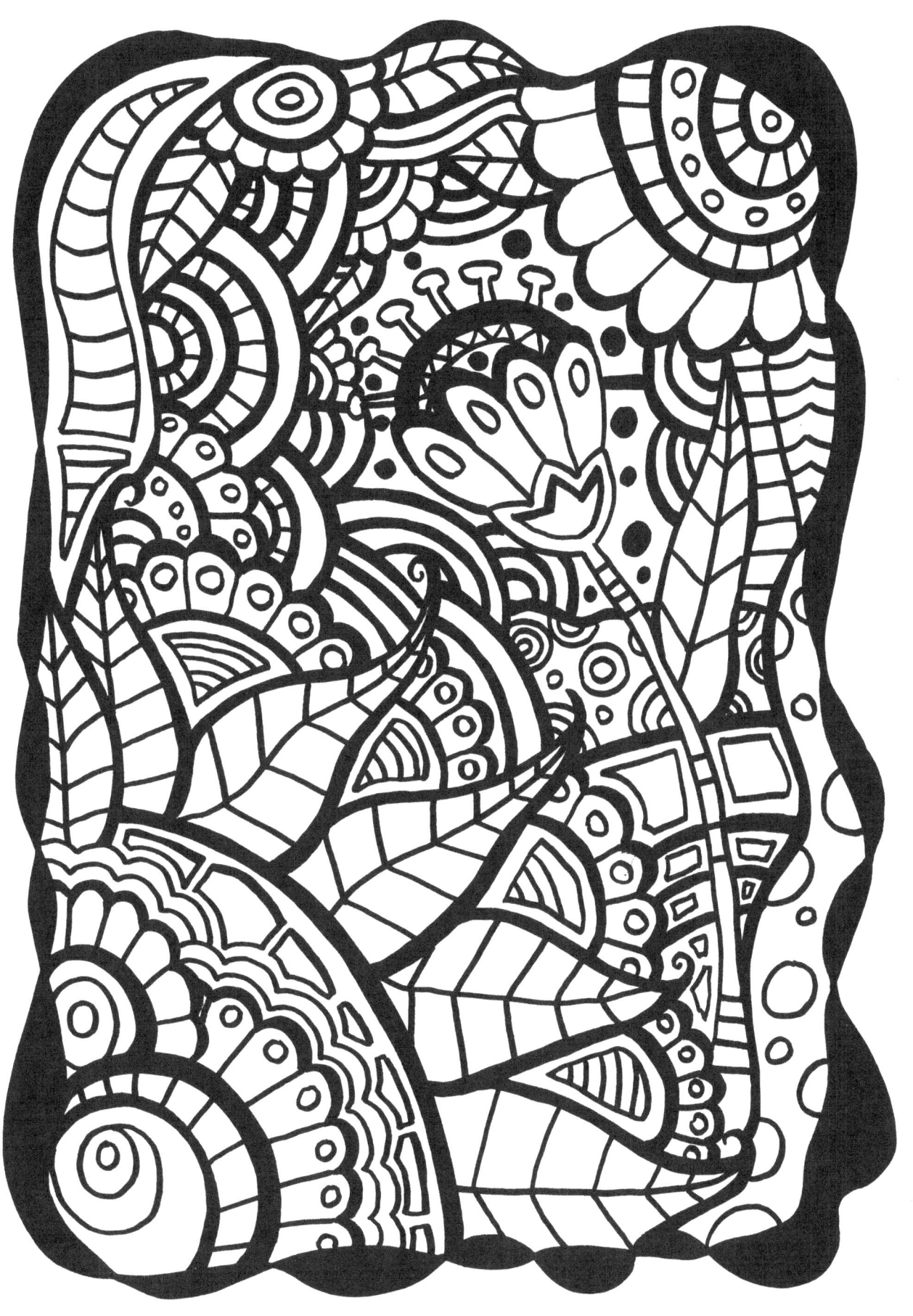

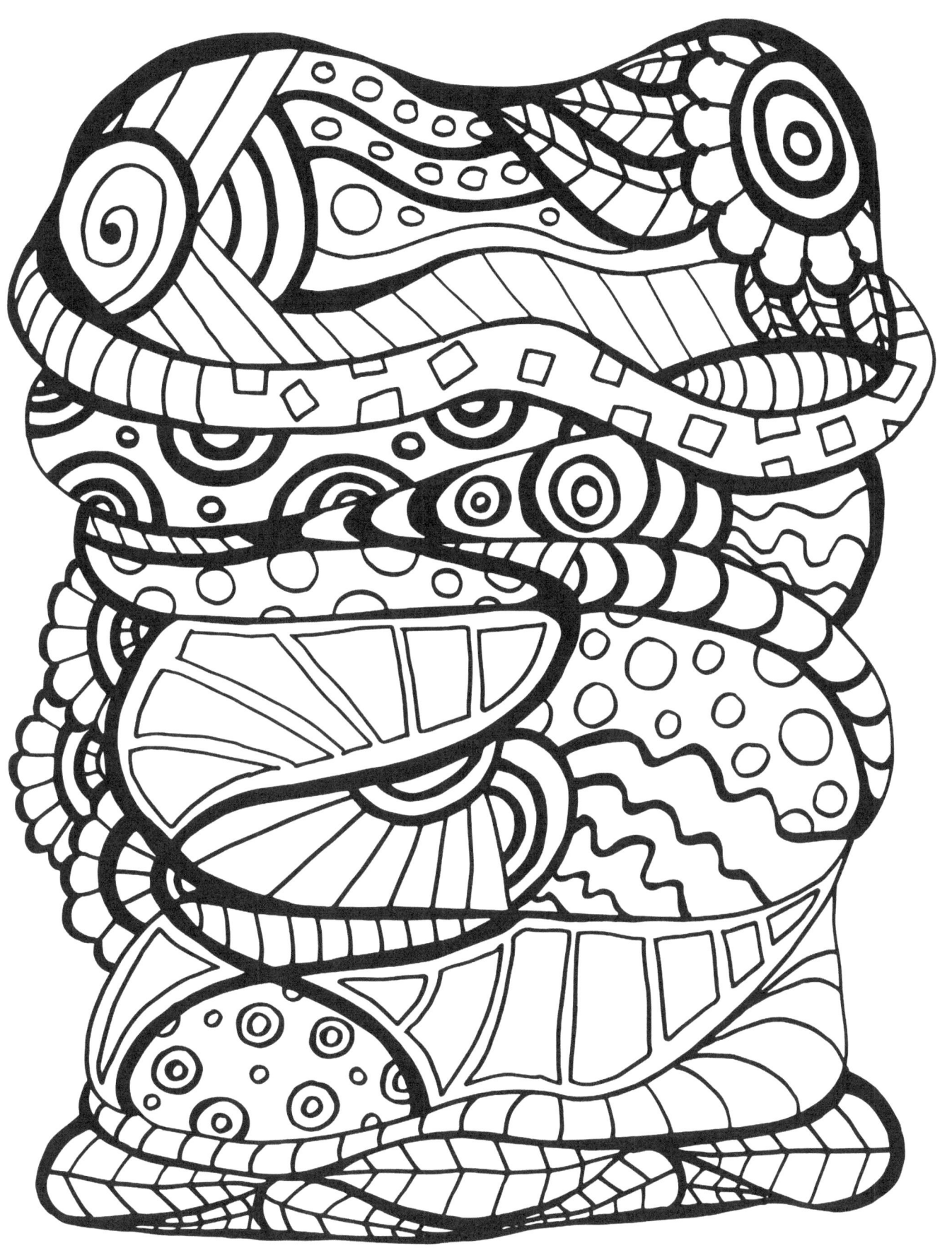

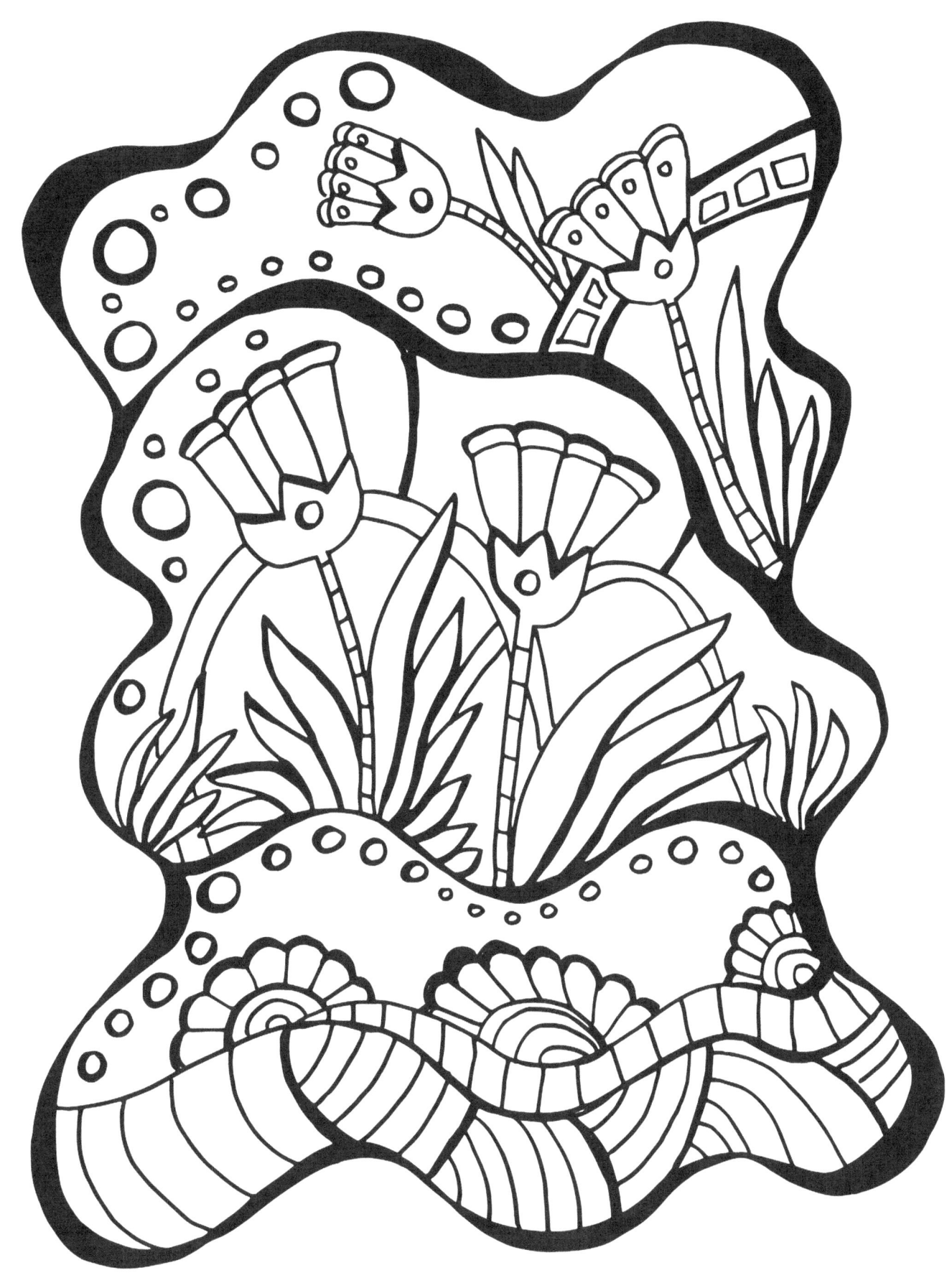

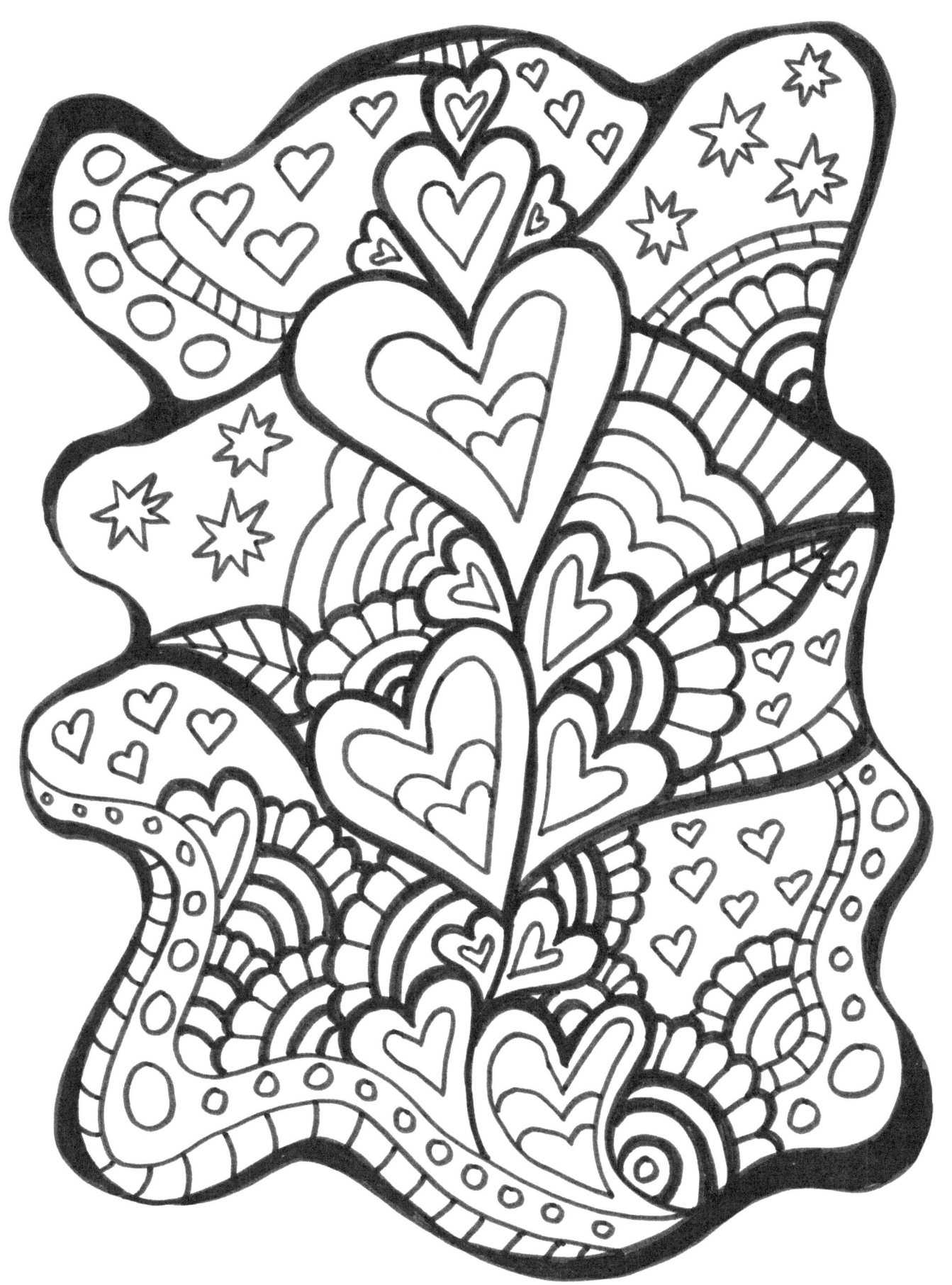

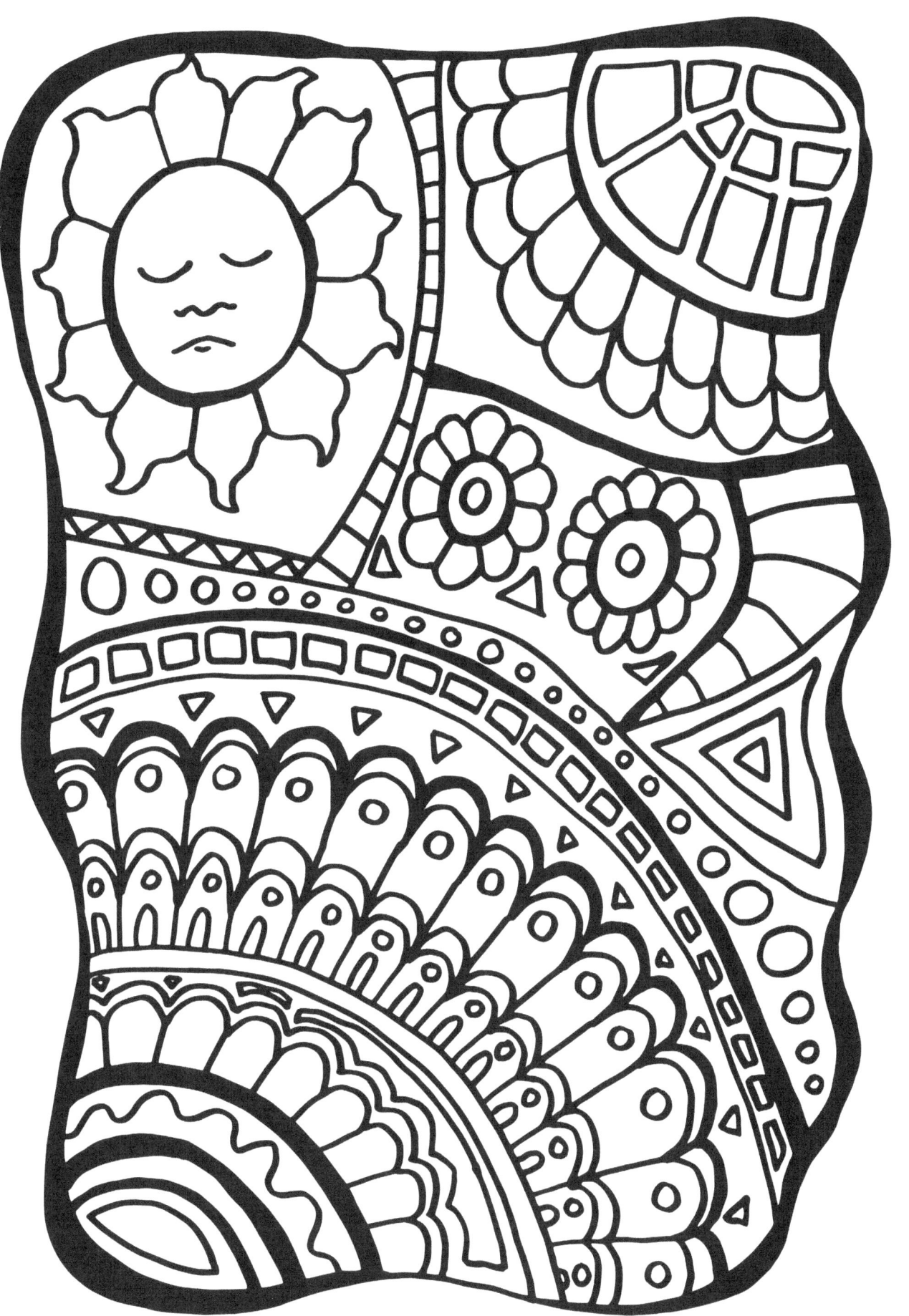

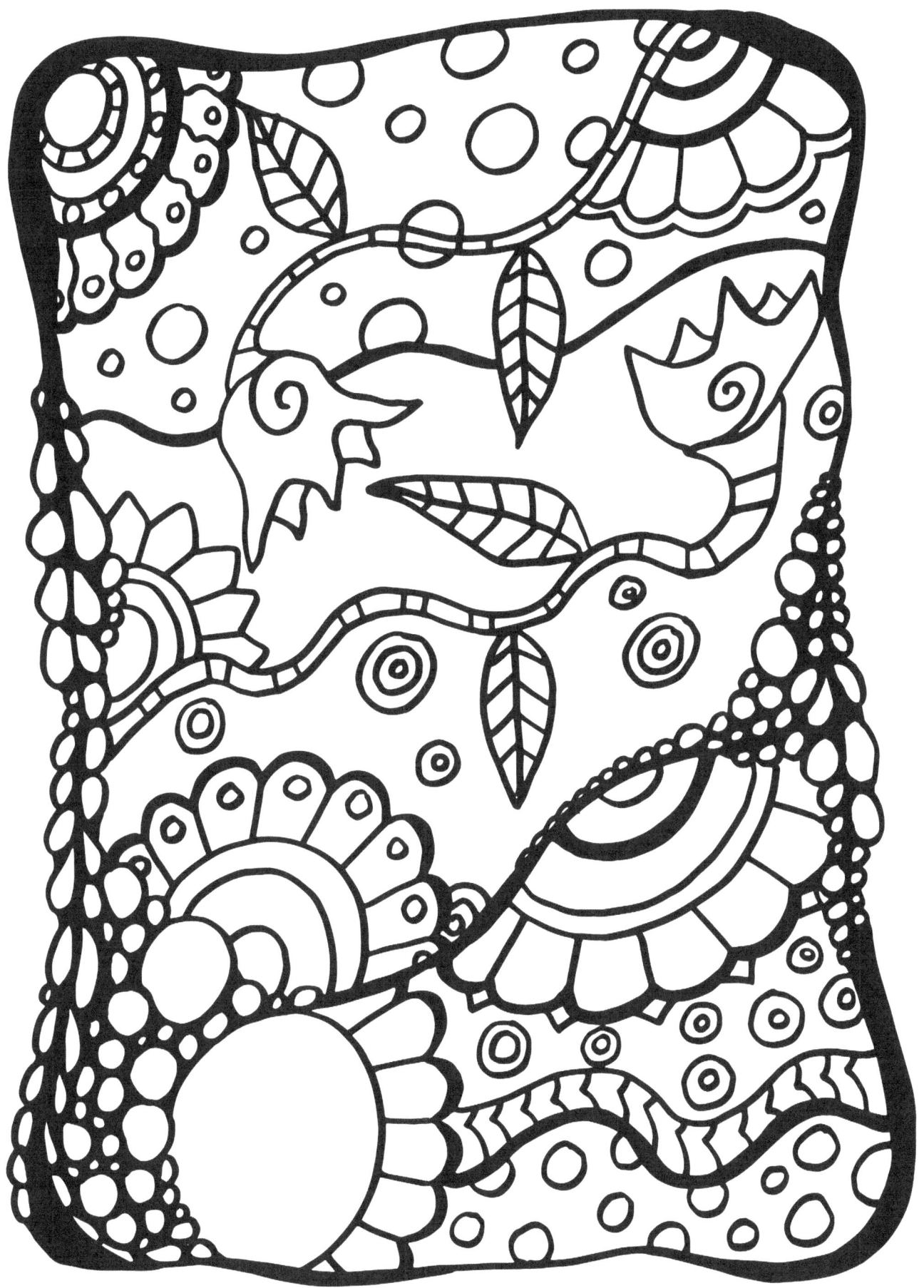

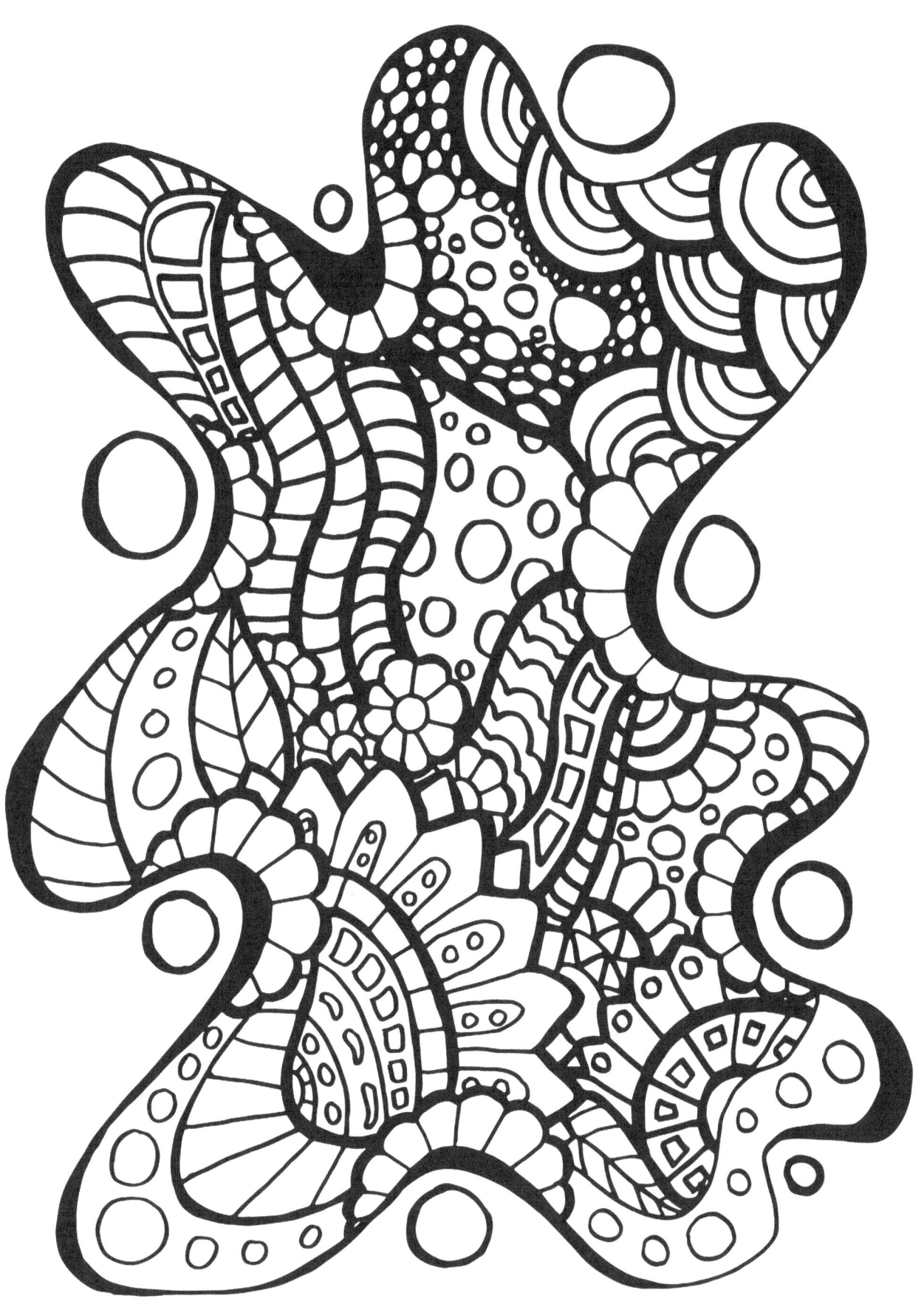

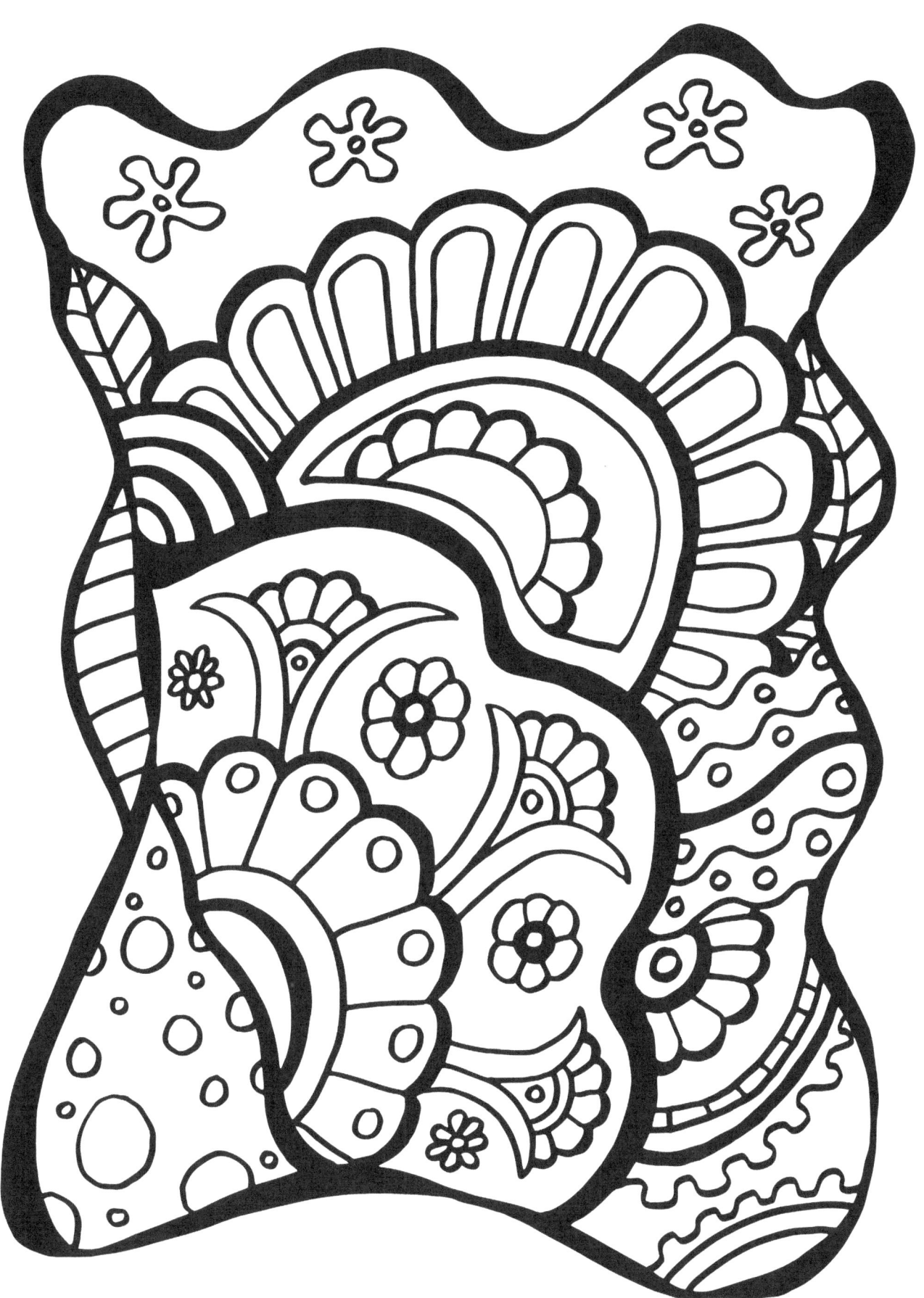

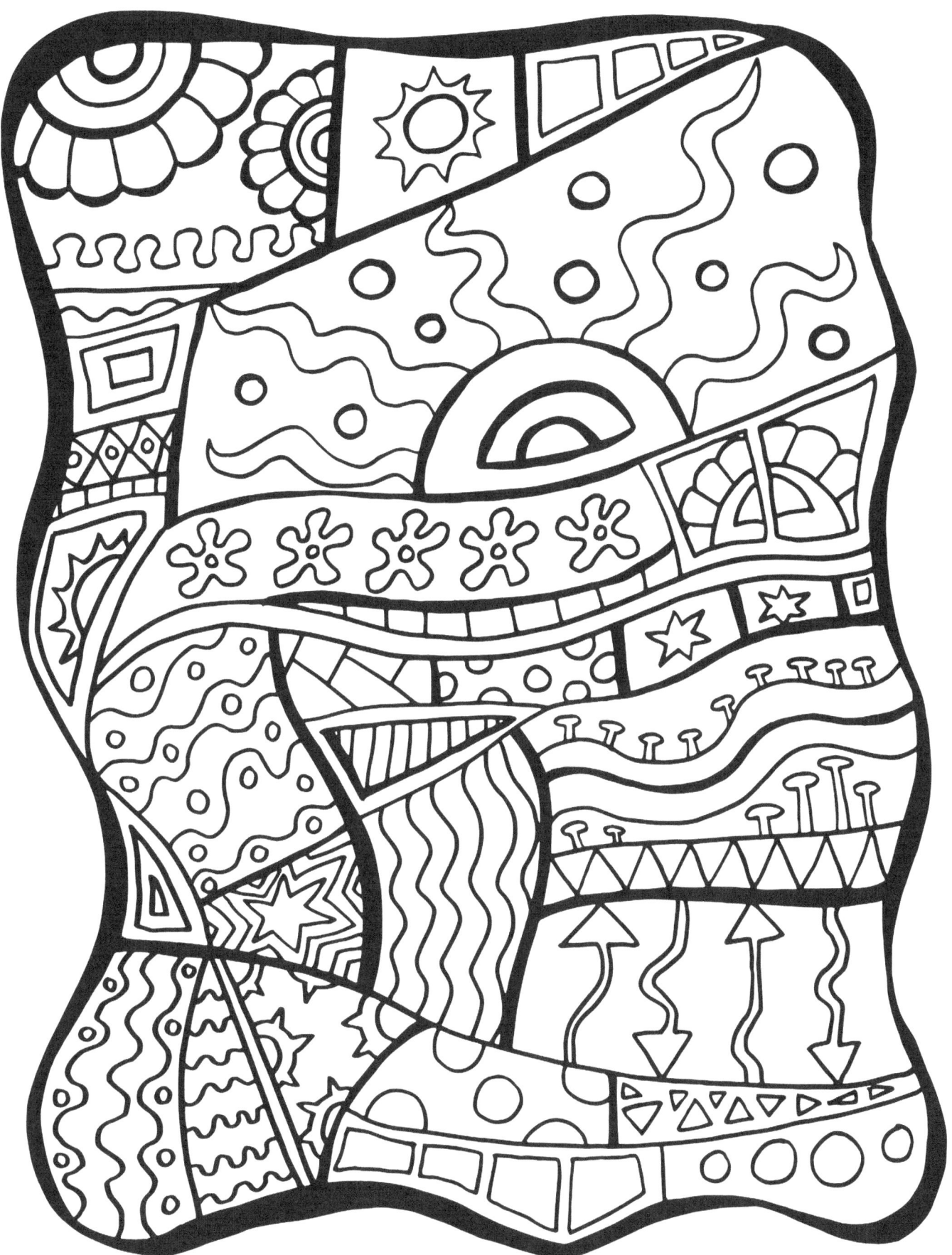

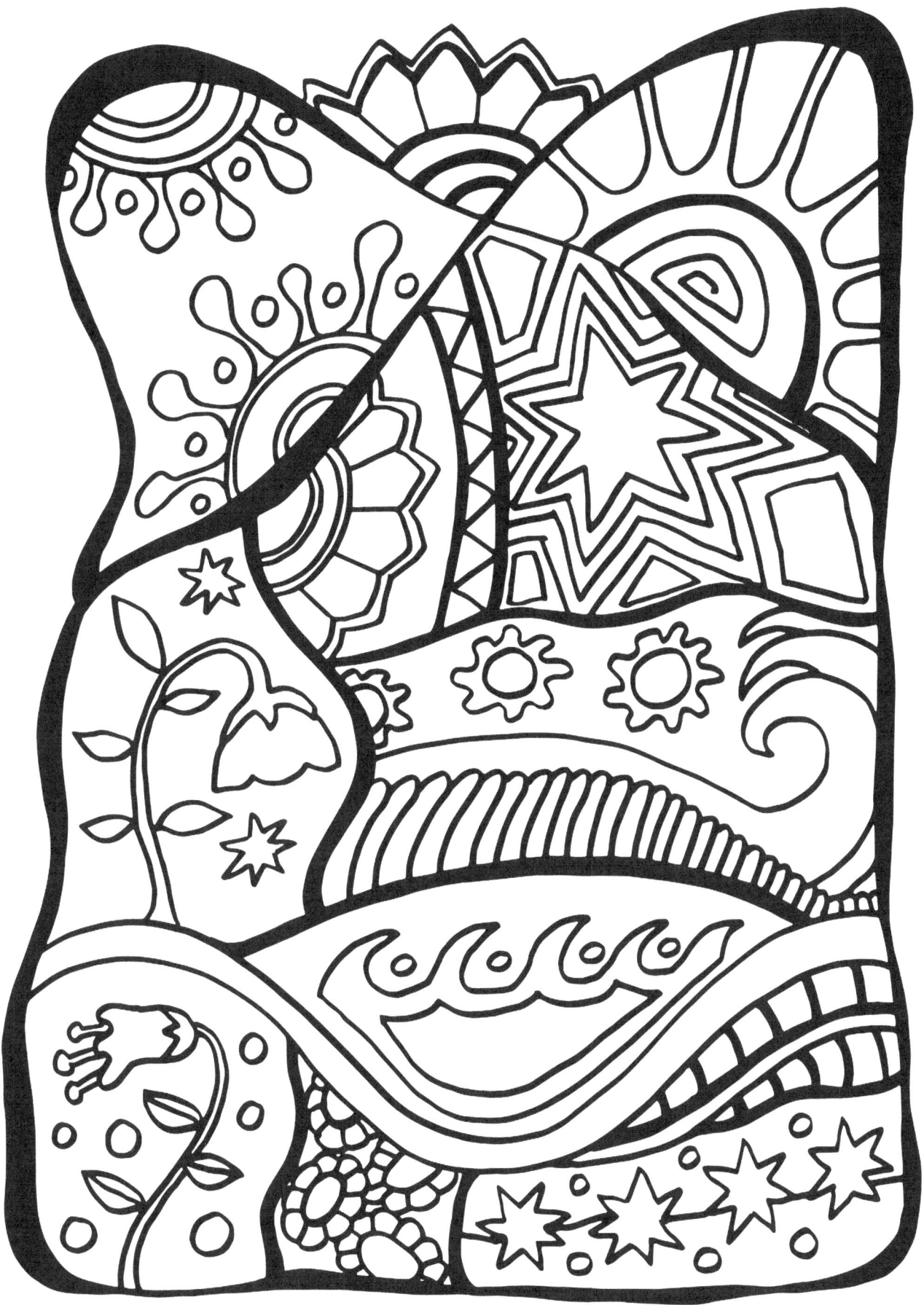

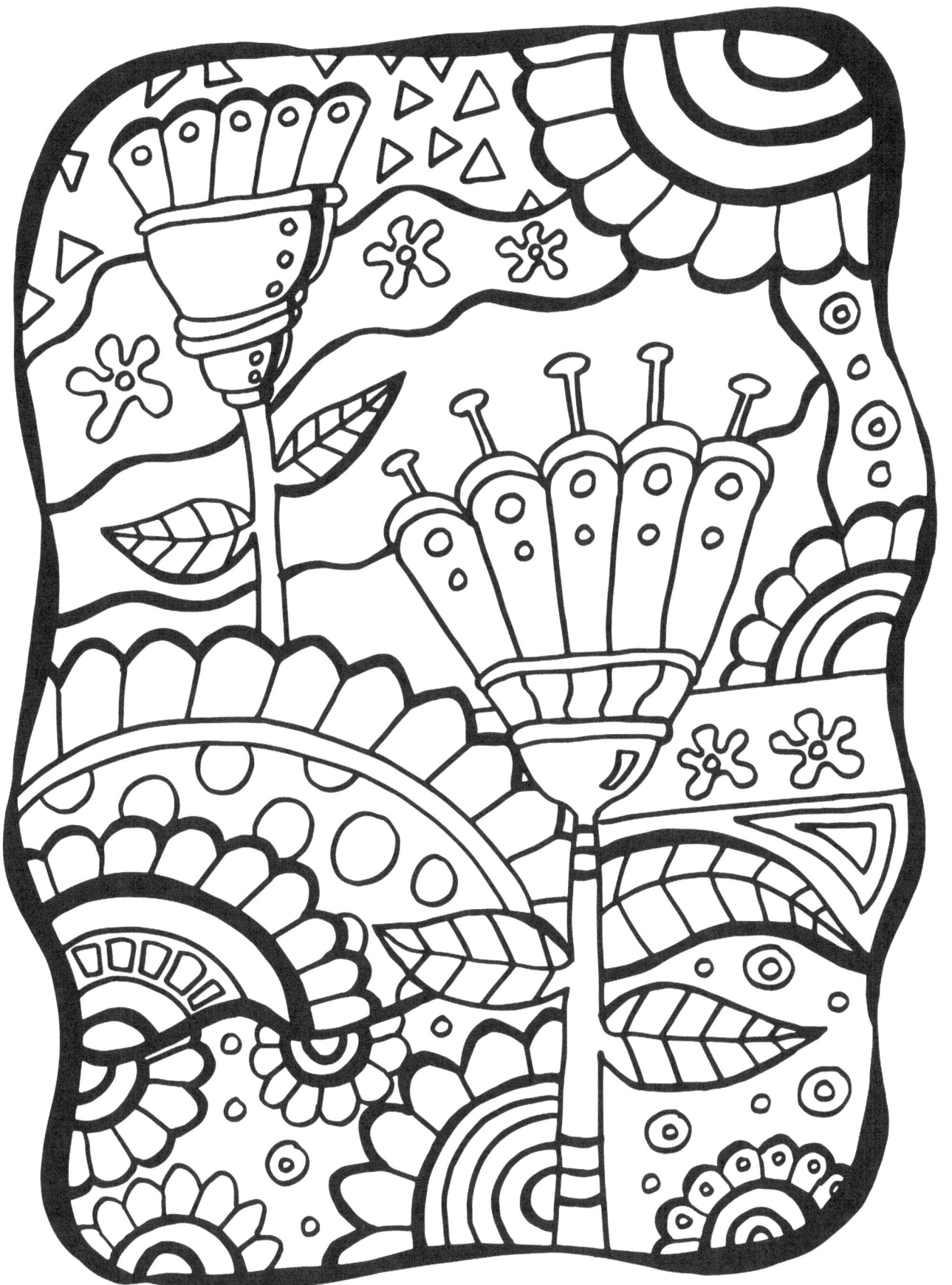

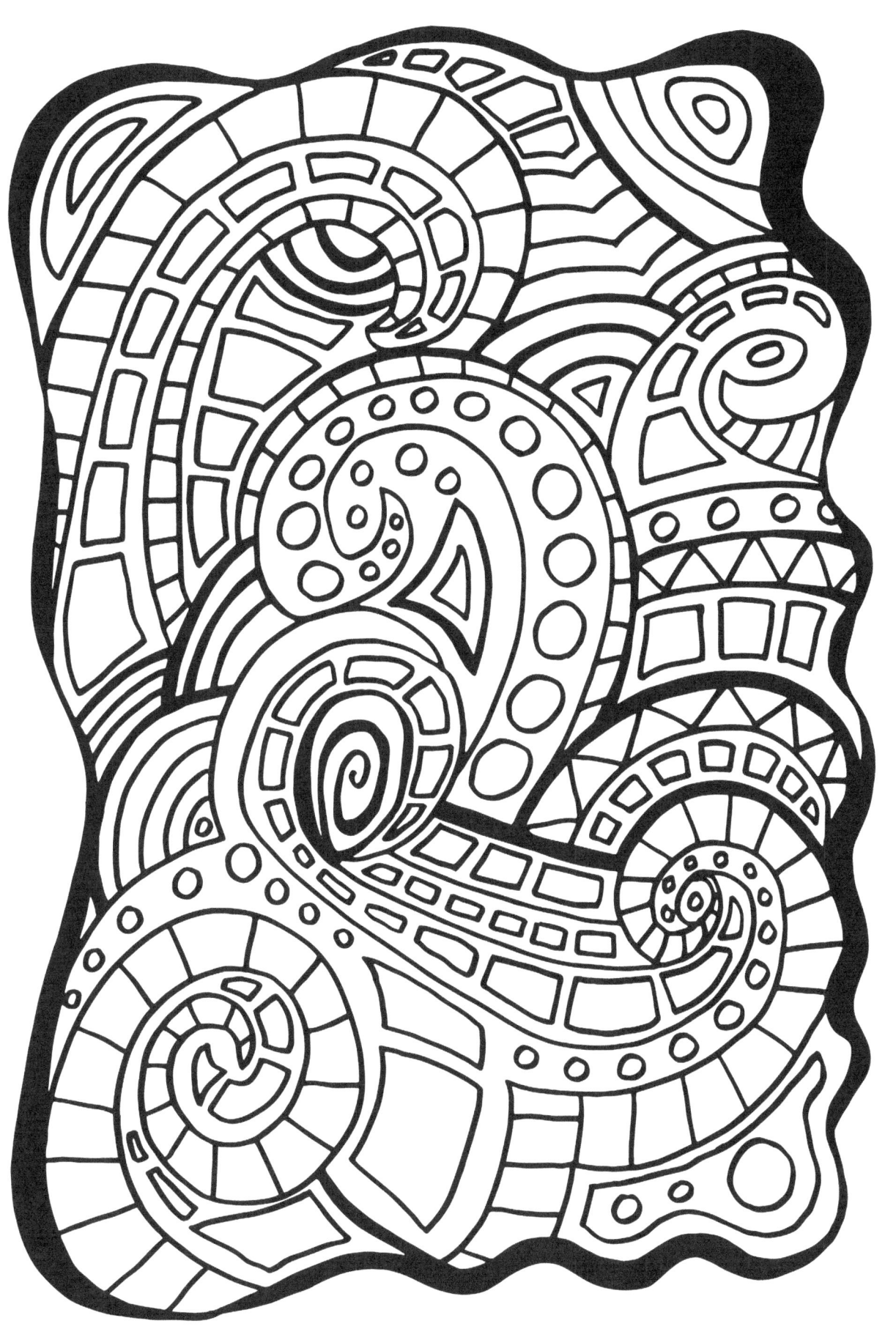

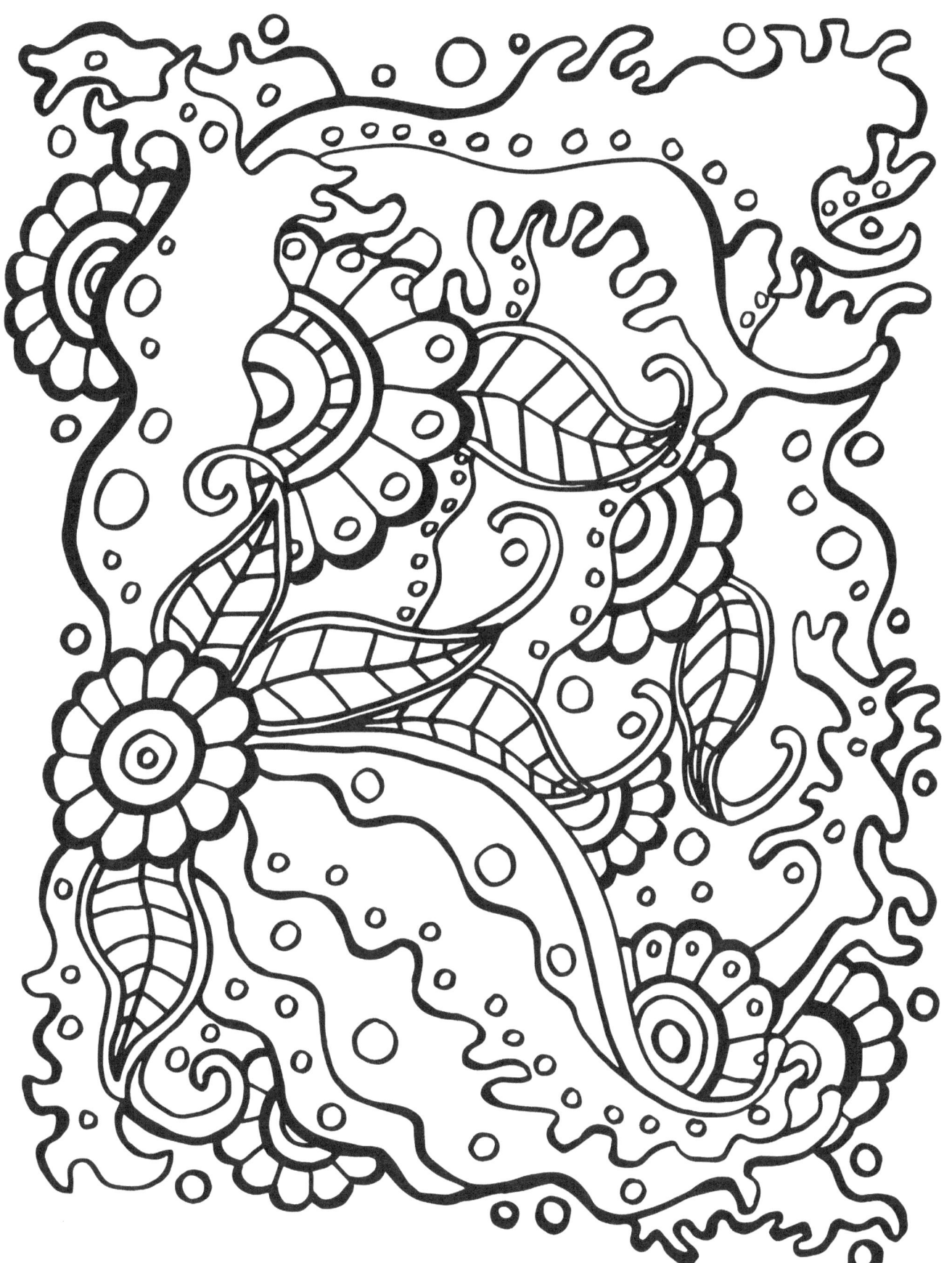

Also Available by Kimberly Garvey

- **Strange Designs** - An adult coloring book for everyone.

- **Strange Little Designs** - A mini/travel adult coloring book.

- **Simple Designs** - An adult coloring book with easier pages.

- **Simple Designs II** - An adult coloring book with easier pages.

- **Simple Little Designs** - A mini/travel sized book w/easier pages.

- **Magical Daydreams** - An adult coloring book for everyone.

- **It's Complicated** - A challenging book for the daring colorists.

- **It's Complicated II -** A more challenging coloring book.

- **The Fox Book** - A foxy coloring book for everyone.

- **SUPER Simple Designs -** SUPER easy adult coloring

- **SUPER Simple Designs II -** Another SUPER easy adult coloring

- **Playful Adventures** - An adult coloring book for everyone.

- **Random Designs** - Designs of various difficulty levels.

- **Alien Flowers From Another Dimension** - A coloring book for everyone.

- **I Love Hearts** - Heart themed coloring book for all.

- **Hours of Flowers** - An adult flowery coloring book.

- **Delightful Journeys**– Landscapes, places and animals.

- **Abstract Painting Coloring Book**— A different kind of grayscale

- **Color a Tree** - Tree themed coloring book.

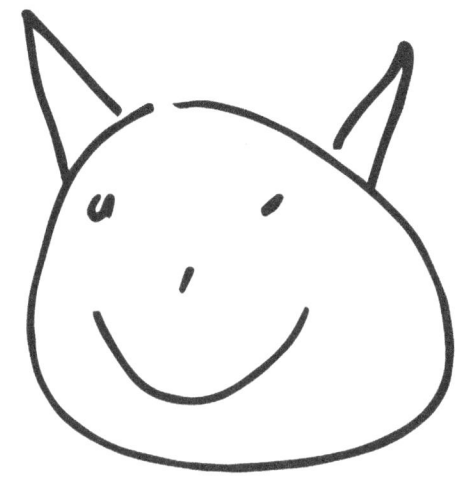

KIMBERLYGARVEY.COM

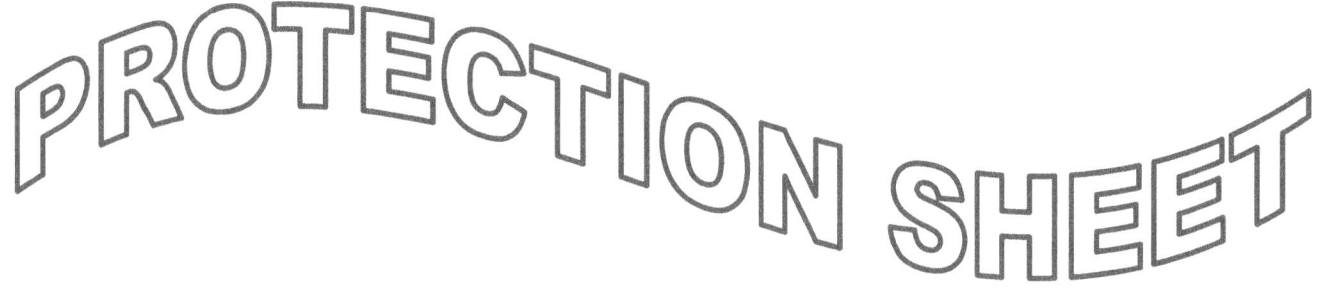

PROTECTION SHEET

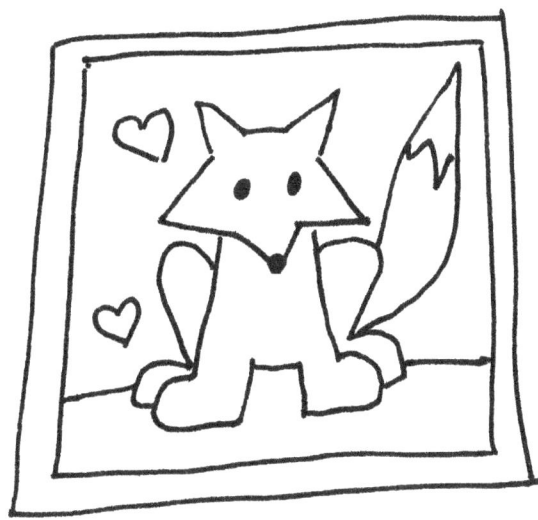

Place this page between coloring

pages when using markers to

prevent bleed-through.

KIMBERLYGARVEY.COM

www.ingramcontent.com/pod-product-compliance
Lightning Source LLC
Chambersburg PA
CBHW081745220526

45468CB00008B/2244